A Woman's World

Beyond the Headlines

Edited by

Mary Van Lieshout

Attic Press & Oxfam
Dublin

First published in 1996 by
Attic Press
29 Upper Mount Street
Dublin 2

and

Oxfam (UK and Ireland)
Oxfam House
274 Banbury Road
Oxford OX2 7DZ

References to the Oxfam programme throughout this book are to the programme of Oxfam (United Kingdom and Ireland).
Oxfam co-publishes this book as a contribution to the understanding of the challenges faced by women around the world. The contributors to *A Woman's World Beyond the Headlines* are entirely responsible for the views and opinions expressed in this book.
Oxfam is registered as charity no. 202918 and in Ireland as charity no. CHY5988.
Oxfam(UK and Ireland) is a member of Oxfam International.

ISBN 1 85594 1 686 Irish Edition
ISBN 0 85598 3 493 UK Edition

A Catalogue record for this title is available from the British Library.

The moral right of individual authors to be identified as authors of this work has been asserted.

Cover Design: Mick O'Dwyer
Cover Illustration: Amanda Brady, Shirley Casey & Catherine Place
Origination: Attic Press
Printing: The Guernsey Press

All photographs reproduced with the kind permission of Oxfam.

Contents

Acknowledgements

After a lifetime of reading books, I had no idea how many people were involved in the production of one. This was clearly a collaborative project and there are many, many people to thank.

First of all, to each of the women who were interviewed for this book, and to all the women who've brought life and depth to these pages by sharing their experiences, very special thanks to each of you from Oxfam UK and Ireland.

Also to President Mary Robinson, for the support, and to each of the authors, special thanks to all of you.

Were it not for the vision and inspiration of Sally Anne Kinahan this project would never have happened in the first place; it never would have been completed without the enormous patience and perseverance of Anne Holmes.

To Caroline Sweetman, of Oxfam's Policy Department and Anna Coryndon of Oxfam Publishing, for the encouragement, clear thinking and expert guidance, how can I ever thank you?

Thanks to the Oxfam staff and partners around the world who've contributed to this book in so many ways. It would be impossible to mention everyone who has helped by hosting journalists, reading and commenting on text, and simply supporting this project.

Particular thanks to the following colleagues and friends who have given so much of their time and energy: Caroline Beadle, Larry Boyd, Tony Burdon, Rob Cornford, Jan Cottell, Dave Dalton, Alison Farrell, Briony Harrison, Tracey Hawkins, Matthew Jowett, Louise Kunzemann, Ian Leggett, Peadar Kirby, Mary McEvoy, Yameema Mitha, Chris Peters, Nick Roseveare, Pat Simmons, Mary Sue Smiaroski, Kate Tarpey, Sarah Totterdell and Pramod Unia.

Thanks to Geraldine Terry for the constant optimism and for the contribution on Sri Lanka; also thanks to Ruth Mayne for the contribution on Chile, an excerpt from her recent report 'Economic Reform and Inequality in Latin America'.

All of us in Oxfam are especially grateful to Róisín Conroy, Ruth Burke Kennedy and the staff at Attic Press for making this project a reality.

To Róisín Ni Cheallaigh, a special thank you for all you do.

Finally, to Brian, Michael, Caitriona and Ciara, my deepest affection and thanks to all of you.

Mary Van Lieshout
April, 1996

Bibi Tura, mother of five, returning home to the village of Chaltapa in the Kilagai area after ten years as a refugee. Previously famed for its melons and watermelons, the village has been stripped of its produce, its wood and the irrigation systems on which local agriculture depended has been destroyed. According to Bibi: 'Before the war, we had a good life here. Whenever we wanted meat we went out and killed a goat. Now we are lucky if we eat meat once a month.' (Meeting Women's Needs: The Challenge of Afghanistan by Ann Kiely)

Photograph by Dianna Melrose.

6

Foreword

The President of Ireland, Mary Robinson

Recognising the concept of a woman's world - as this book does - is in itself valuable. It encourages a globalisation of a whole range of issues. It transcends the enormous difference between standards of living and lifestyles of women in the developed world and developing countries, and indeed between rich and poor in developed regions. So what does it mean? It may not amount to much more than acknowledgement of a bond, an empathy, an instinctive recognition of a similar way of responding to immediate practical problems. It evokes some shared element of experience - however different the context - of being excluded, marginalised, discriminated against, victimised, undervalued. It includes frustration about unrealised potential, energies dissipated, impotence in the face of established structures. It often manifests itself in shared humour, self-expression through song and dance, and the sheer 'buzz' evident at gatherings such as the Beijing Conference.

Let me put a human face on all of this. As part of the preparation for the Beijing Conference a number of women's organisations in Ireland, North and South, contributed patches for a quilt to symbolise the activities and links of women's groups on the island of Ireland. Subsequently, the women who had brought the quilt to Beijing, and representatives of the women's groups involved, came to visit me at Aras an Uachtaráin. There were several parts of their story which encapsulated for me that sense of a woman's world. Firstly, the inclusiveness of the groups who participated: urban and rural, North and South, young and less young, traveller women, women in prison. Secondly, their capacity to listen and learn. They told me of how they were influenced by the approach of women from developing countries towards stifling administrative regulations. If it makes no sense, ignore it! The example they gave was the proposed location of the market area to allow women to sell crafts and goods they had brought with them. The designated zone was tucked away at the back, but since selling was essential to funding the stay of many women a central location was taken over for the market and became a vibrant arena of exchange. They also described how they had paraded the Irish quilt along the streets, singing and dancing, and were pleased to hear the comment that Irish women seemed more like women from Africa or South America than from western Europe!

7

One of the positive developments during the decade between Nairobi and Beijing has been the flourishing of women's networks North and South. A growing number of women have linked together across borders, class and race to struggle jointly towards an alternative vision of society. The Irish women's network, Banúlacht, expresses this new understanding through its work helping our local community-based women's groups gain a greater understanding of development issues. By organising training workshops, conferences and linking women from different parts of the world in discussions of common problems Banúlacht provides a useful role model for women in other countries. I know that women from the Third World who have come to Ireland to share their experiences with women's groups here have both contributed and benefitted enormously.

I welcome the publication of this book under the auspices of Oxfam and Attic Press, based on the work of women journalists, development practitioners and academics documenting the role and experience of women in developing countries during the year of the UN conference on women in Beijing. These women who have been outside history are now given a voice.

The women who have contributed to this publication challenge us in their writings. We must respond to that challenge.

Mary Robinson

Introduction

Mary Van Lieshout

'The majority of women have suffered profoundly; we have suffered in our bodies - through blows, starvation, rape, infection ... and in our hearts. Every day is a struggle against hunger or madness. The two torment us. To survive we have formed small self-help organisations which allow us to look for solutions to material problems, while at the same time giving each other moral support to carry on.'[1]

There were many global events that shaped the international agenda in 1995, and with them, individual lives will be changed forever. In Africa, East African communities and governments struggled to find a sustainable peace and justice for the region in the aftermath of the genocide in 1994 which claimed over a million lives in Rwanda. A fragile cease-fire held in Northern Ireland; war raged throughout the year in the Balkans and Caucasia.

There were other anniversaries, and commemorations, less traumatic, but also with far reaching implications. The United Nations celebrated its fiftieth anniversary, and two of its sister agencies, the World Bank and the International Monetary Fund turned fifty-one, in spite of a campaign called 'Fifty Years is Enough' by non-governmental organisations (NGOs) targeted at the institutions.

Another Bretton Woods institution, the General Agreement on Tariffs and Trade, which for decades governed international trade relations, gave birth on 1 January to the World Trade Organisation. This closely followed the 1994 agreement between the USA, Canada and Mexico - the North American Free Trade Agreement - which created the world's largest free trade zone.

1995 was also the year of the Fourth World Conference on Women. To observe the Year, the United Nations Development Programme focused its annual report on the situation of women. While the report recorded significant gains for women, including an important increase in female literacy globally, there was also some devastating news. The face of poverty and destitution is increasingly female: seventy per cent of the world's absolute poor are women. Violence against the girl child - female infanticide and neglect - continues unabated, and, worldwide, males receive twice as many years of schooling as their female counterparts.[2]

Ten years after the 'Decade for Women' closed, women around the world soberly prepared to address the issues at the Fourth World Conference on Women, held in Beijing in September, with the theme of

'Action for Peace, Equality and Development'.

Oxfam chose to commemorate the Beijing Conference by commissioning the collection of articles that make up this book. We sought to capture and record the achievements and daily heroism, as well as the protest that is alive in small communities, in grassroots groups and in the individual women with whom we work throughout the world.

The media and the stories which make it to our newspaper pages and television news are the basis for most people's understanding of developing countries. However, behind and beyond the headlines, there are, of course, other stories. Stories which are sensational only in that they expose tremendous fortitude and courage, and gross exploitation and denial of human rights.

This theme, women's daily fight for basic rights, and their challenge to global poverty and violence, is the focus of *A Woman's World*. In the following sections, the contributions explore the implications of conflict, economic adjustment and development policies for women in Southern countries.

Helen O'Connell introduces the theme of the globalisation of world markets and its impact on women. Today products, money and information criss-cross the world at lightning speed with little regard for national boundaries. The new rules on world trade in financial investment and information will give an extra boost to this process, further undermining the rights of national governments to protect local industries and jobs. Globalisation has meant that 'measures aimed at protecting the livelihoods, health and future of poor people - laws on minimum wages, workers' rights and environmental protection - are under attack, as transnational corporations (TNCs) move production and jobs from one country to another in a restless search for minimum restraint and maximum profitability'.[3]

O'Connell describes structural adjustment programmes: a combination of public expenditure cutbacks, tight money controls, and market deregulation which aim to restore viability to deeply indebted economies. Third World countries, now indebted to the tune of £115 billion[4] must, as a precondition for new loans from Northern donors, implement this package of economic reforms. However, fifteen years on, adjustment is widely criticised for its impact on social welfare and in many countries poverty has deepened.

It is widely acknowledged that poor communities have suffered most under fast-paced economic reform, which has undermined local jobs and access to health and education. Some argue that cuts in public expenditure and welfare spending are made with the deliberate expectation that women will increase their work as providers of health and social services.[5]

Siobhán Creaton traces the impact of 'free trade' and the liberalisation of trade rules in Chile, now the world's largest supplier of seasonal fruit to the northern hemisphere. Creaton found a 'two track' system, one overworked, grossly underpaid and overwhelmingly female, and another which has gained the material benefits of free trade.

As Chile prepares to join the North American Free Trade Agreement, which will further undermine local industry and workers rights, Creaton found women trade unionists worried and wary about the future. Ruth Mayne focuses her attention on the meaning of 'flexibility' for Chile's working women.

Trish Hegarty examines the Ugandan Health Care system and notes how past conflict and current poverty have combined to erode the quality of what was once one of Africa's finest health systems. Hegarty describes how restrictions imposed on government spending under the structural adjustment programme have undermined the government's ability to develop and resource public health programmes.

The Economist has heralded Uganda as one of a few structural adjustment success stories.[6] However, as Hegarty found, the cost of Uganda's modest success is borne heavily by women and, increasingly by children. She found inadequate health services concentrated in the urban areas and scarce in rural Uganda. She follows the debate on user fees for health, and visits a number of child headed households, parentless due to the AIDS crisis.

Uganda's debt is peculiar in that a high proportion of the repayments go to international financial institutions, such as the World Bank and the IMF, which are financed by Northern taxpayers. Hegarty argues for cancellation of the debt to enable the Ugandan government to redirect resources into health care systems for its people.

When the new president of the World Bank, James Wolfensohn, addressed a gathering of women activists at the UN Conference in Beijing, he promised a 'new Bank ... a Bank ready to listen, to change'. Watkins acknowledges, that while the World Bank now attempts to protect essential state services, such as health care, during economic reform, these attempts are 'so far without much obvious success'.[7]

The second section of the book deals with the issue of conflict and its impact on women. War and conflict pose an ever increasing threat to development, robbing communities and families of their livelihoods, homes and emotional and material security. All but two of the 127 armed conflicts which happened in the world between 1945 and 1989 took place in the South.[8] During World War II, fifty-two per cent of war-related deaths were among civilians. Today four out of every five casualties are civilians, most of them women and children.[9]

Breeda Hickey, who worked with Oxfam in Rwanda from 1993-1995, describes the challenges facing Rwandan women in the aftermath of the genocide. She describes the physical and emotional toll the conflict has taken, as women struggle to find economic security for their families, and come to terms with the loss of family and friends in such violent circumstances. Sexual violence and rape were used in Rwanda, as elsewhere, as weapons of war. Rape during conflict is now widely recognised 'as a routine way of terrorising and humiliating women, and often, through them, their entire ethnic group'.[10]

While Hickey focuses mainly on the impact of the Rwandan genocide on women, she outlines in her introduction the global and pervasive nature of violence against women 'in the home and often at the hands of those we trust'.

Róisín Boyd and Maggie O'Kane visit communities in the process of 'reconstruction' and describe the challenges that remain long after conflict has ended. From Cambodia to the Philippines to Mozambique, when women are rebuilding homes or searching for the graves of loved ones they suffer material disadvantage and physical relocation as the natural and direct results of conflict. In Mozambique and Cambodia thousands of hidden landmines remain and continue to wreak havoc in individual lives long after a peace has been declared.

From Pakistan, Aileen O'Meara charts the rise of Islamisation, used now as a tool to oppress women and curtail their freedom. O'Meara describes the ordinances of General Zia-ul Haq during the period of martial law which ran from 1977 to 1985[11] which continue to influence and shape women's lives. While O'Meara spoke to many women actively campaigning against the Islamisation movement, Uzma Pirzada, who works in a literacy project in Pakistan stresses that 'spirituality is important for people: they do not see Islam as oppressive'. This highlights the need for clarity in discussions about the relationship between religion, spirituality and fundamentalist movements.[12]

Women Against Fundamentalism (WAF) defines fundamentalism as 'modern political movements which use religion as a basis for their attempt to win or consolidate power and extend social control', a definition which can usefully be applied to movements far beyond Islamic states.[13]

O'Meara meets human rights campaigners, artists and NGOs, and encounters diverse views on the future of Pakistan under the leadership of Benazir Bhutto.

The final section of the book focuses on development strategies to combat the 'feminisation' of poverty and exclusion demonstrated in the first two sections. Mary Jennings outlines the early development approaches which attempted to focus on women, including the (still common) approach of policy makers referred to as 'women in development' (WID) where the aim of development interventions is 'increased productivity and welfare'.[14] The failure of this approach, according to Peggy Antrobus, is the premise that women had to be 'integrated into development' ... as if they could possibly exist 'outside the process'.[15]

Jennings goes on to describe the 'Gender and Development' analysis (GAD), where policy interventions are designed in the light of men's and women's socially constructed roles and responsiblities, and a fundamental aim of development policy is 'increased participation and equality'.[16] With evidence from a wide range of countries, Jennings highlights the challenges that face the international community in moving from the theory to the practice of gender-aware development strategies.

Deirdre Considine and Ann Kiely describe Oxfam interventions in two countries where ongoing conflict creates a context of 'semi-permanent emergency'. These long-running conflicts have all but fallen from the pages of our newspapers, and their victims are largely ignored by the media and the international community alike.

At least one million people have died in the conflict in Sudan, with a further 1.5 million driven from their homes into camps, or across borders. The conflict has led to a dramatic reduction in women's support systems and has threatened their ability to support their children and families. In the context of reduced health and education systems, Considine highlights the importance of, and some problems encountered in, gender sensitive approaches in the transition from relief to development work.

Ann Kiely admits the difficulties in developing an appropriate response to 'meet women's needs' in the midst of extreme vulnerability and uncertainty in Kabul, the capital of Afghanistan. She cites Oxfam research with over 800 women in the city, who identified childcare, literacy classes, income generation, and health clinics as their immediate priorities. Kiely describes the tenacity and resourcefulness of the Kabul women in securing an income, but notes that 'many were dependent solely on their young children going out and peddling every day'.

The Beijing Conference and the women who created it run as threads through the whole book. Lorna Siggins elaborates on the conference and some of the individuals and issues that generated the energy that was unique to the gathering. She focuses on the single minded courage of Mary McGoldrick of Dublin and others who told their stories at the International Tribunal on Women's Human Rights held in Beijing. Siggins reviews the Beijing Conference Document and its eleven 'critical areas of concern' for women, and describes the accomplishment, the controversies, and the unfinished business of Beijing.

Maude Mugisha, chairperson of the Ugandan Women's Network tells Penny Cabot of Banúlacht about the priorities of Ugandan women in Beijing and their hopes for the conference.

Cidia Monteiro, of Forum Mulher, the Association of Women's NGOs in Mozambique contributes an excerpt from their submission to Beijing, which describes the situation of women in Mozambique, and priorities for action.

These women were among the thousands who worked for years prior to the Beijing conference to develop strategies to ensure that the conference document, the 'Platform for Action', would accurately represent women's gains and achievements and identify clearly the obstacles to peace, development and equality. It is clear now that the real test of Beijing will be in the implementation of the outlined strategies: will governments keep their promises? Will we as activists hold them accountable?

The agenda for change is enormous and the central challenge remains meeting the needs of the grassroots women speaking in this book, whose lives are shaped by decisions taken in remote institutions and processes. Certainly the programme must include a radically reformed United Nations: one which has preventative diplomacy as a central priority. Resources to pursue conflict prevention are critical. Openness and responsive economic policies from the Bretton Woods institutions - the World Bank, the International Monetary Fund and the World Trade Organisation - are also critical if we are to end the escalation of poverty and marginalisation.

These 'macro-issues' of economic policy, trade liberalisation, conflict and its resolution have tremendous impact on the daily lives of women everywhere.

Peggy Antrobus, of Development Alternatives for Women in a New Era (DAWN), sets the initial ground rules for the programme of change: 'the analysis should be one which attempts to relate experience at the microlevel of the sector, community, project, or household, to that of macro-economic analysis'.[17]

And the Platform For Action from the Beijing Conference sets out clearly our final goal: 'A transformed partnership based on equality between women and men ... in the home, in the work place and in the wider national and international communities.'[18]

NOTES:
1. Esther Mujawayo, Kigali, Rwanda. December 1995.
2. Human Development Report, United Nations Development Programme, 1995.
3. Simmons, P *Words Into Action*, Oxfam Publications, 1995.
4. Dalton, D *Rights Now*, Oxfam Publications, 1995.
5. Elson, D in *World Bank Structural Adjustment and Gender Policies*
    EURODAD/WIDE Position Paper, Sept. 1994.
6. *The Economist*, 21 - 27 October, 1995.
7. Watkins, K *The Oxfam Poverty Report*, Oxfam Publications, 1995.
8. The Oxfam Report, *It's Time For a Fairer World*, Oxfam Publications, 1991.
9. Watkins, op.cit.
10. Simmons, op.cit.
11. Choudhury, Golam. *Pakistan. Transition from Military to Civil Rule*,
    Scorpion Publishing, 1988.
12. Sweetman, C in *Focus on Gender*, 'Women and Culture' Oxfam
    Publications, 1995.
13. *Women Against Fundamentalism*, 129 Seven Sisters Road, London. Publicity
    literature, 1994.

14. Hlupekile Llongwe, S 'Gender Awareness, The Missing Element in Third World Development Project', in *Changing Perceptions*, Wallace, T (ed), Oxfam Publications, 1991.
15. Antrobus, P 'Women in Development' in *Changing Perceptions*, Wallace, T (ed), Oxfam Publications, 1991.
16. Hlupekile Llongwe, S. op.cit.
17. Antrobus, P. op.cit.
18. The Platform For Action, Fourth World Conference on Women, September 1995.

Mariam Dem, Oxfam programme coordinator in Senegal at the Oxfam workshop 'Beyond the 20th Century: the challenges for women-centered development co-operation'. Beijing, September 1995. (The Fourth World Conference on Women: Beyond the Headlines by Lorna Siggins)

Photograph by Nancy Durrell McKenna.

The Fourth World Conference on Women: Beyond the Headlines

Lorna Siggins

In September, 1995, Mary McGoldrick took a flight home to Dublin from China. On a stretcher. She barely remembers the journey. For most of the trip, she was tranquilised. She had no silk scarves in her suitcase. No souvenirs of an eventful time. On one trip out to the Great Wall, she drew her breath at the wild and wonderful view along the tumbling ramparts; and at a wasp close by. She dodged, heard the crunch, and doubled up with agonizing pain. It was a chronic back injury returning to haunt her. It would be a month or more before she would be able to survive without medication, and weeks before she could think again.

A few days before her mishap, the thirty-five-year-old mother of three from Neilstown, west Dublin, had stood up in front of a packed audience of people who had travelled to China from all over the world to attend the United Nations fourth world conference on women. Speaking at the 'alternative' conclave - the non-governmental organisation (NGO) forum in Huairou, thirty miles outside Beijing - Mary had recounted how she sustained the back injury in the first place. Six years ago, she had secured a barring order against her husband. Mary was a victim of domestic violence.

She talked of how she had met her husband when she was fourteen years old. How she fell in love with him, became pregnant and was married at seventeen. How in 1977, when she was seven months pregnant, her husband went missing for a weekend and she reported him to the police. How when he returned, she told him what she had done and he chased her up the stairs.

How the marriage would never be the same again. Before her second child, she had been attacked. It would continue after the birth of her daughter in 1978. A social worker sent her to a hostel for the homeless run by the Catholic church. 'I remember vividly walking down the street to the hostel with one baby in my arms and holding one by the hand and a bag that I had packed in a hurry,' she told her audience in the Huairou cinema. 'I was nineteen. When I saw all the people sitting along the road outside the hostel drinking bottles of wine, I was too scared to bring my children into that place.

'I went to a church to feed my baby and to get out of the cold. I knew it was useless to think that I could make it on my own with two babies and no money. I had no choice but to go home.'

There would be more blows, punches, kicks, severe beatings: a pot of boiling water was thrown at her at one stage. On another occasion, her husband banged a door against her head. He left the family home for a while, she struggled to keep three children fed; when she did seek a barring order, custody of the children and maintenance, she found that she had to enforce the law herself.

Mary had to collect her maintenance from his place of work; the custody order allowed her husband access and he would keep the children out till all hours, worrying her sick; the barring order was 'not much use when he arrived at midnight and I had no phone to call the police'.

'One night I came home and found him in my bed,' she told the tribunal, hosted by the Centre for Women's Global Leadership of Rutgers University in New Jersey. 'My babysitter had been too afraid to stop him coming in. I rang the police from a friend's house and they came and told him to leave. I did not realise at the time that the police should have arrested my husband and charged him with breaking a court order.'

Her barring order expired after twelve months. She was told that she could not renew it unless she had 'fresh evidence' of abuse. Like bruises, cuts, broken bones. 'The Irish government has never treated his actions as a serious crime,' she said of the situation in which her husband was never prosecuted. He eventually began a relationship with another woman, who has two children by him now. 'He is never asked if he is Miss, Mrs or Ms. He is always Mr in the eyes of the world.

Mary McGoldrick is, as she said herself, a survivor. Other survivors recounted their harrowing experiences to the tribunal. An American woman had killed her husband in self defence. There were accounts of the effect of Muslim fundamentalism in Algeria and Bangladesh. Zazi Sadou, spokeswoman for an Algerian resistance movement, testified on detention camps run by fundamentalists in which women and girls are enslaved and coerced into 'temporary marriages' known as mutaa.

Two Rwandan women, Felicite Umutanguha and Bernadette Kanzayire, testified on war crimes in Rwanda, while a case delivered on behalf of a Chilean woman, known only as Maria, described how she had survived an involuntary hysterectomy, the amputation of her arm, psychological and verbal abuse in a public hospital and imprisonment. All because she needed to terminate a pregnancy in a Catholic state where abortion is a crime.

The culmination of a series of such hearings at previous UN conferences, the tribunal aimed to increase UN awareness of violations of women's human rights. Women had reached a crossroads, the tribunal stated. Their role in society might be growing, but documented violations had never been greater. At the UN world conference on human rights in Vienna, Austria, in 1993, 171 member states had adopted a declaration and programme for action which stated that 'the human rights of women should form an integral part of the UN activities'.

Mary McGoldrick's case would be one of three examined in greater depth by a legal team, to determine ways in which the Irish government, as a UN member, could be challenged and held account-able.

Domestic violence was firmly on the Beijing agenda.

Why Beijing? It was a question that would be asked time and again before the NGO forum and the official UN conference were over. Was this a sop to one of the organisation's five permanent members in compensation for China's failure to secure the 2000 Olympic Games? A way to ease the path of the world's fastest growing economy into membership of the World Trade Organisation? In a country where feudal foot-binding had been replaced by a one-child policy, and Mao Zedong's proclamation that women held up half the sky?

If it was any of these - and truth was that Beijing had already been fixed as the venue before the Olympic decision was made - the Chinese government almost made a mess of it. There was the controversial relocation of the NGO forum, the 'alternative' conference, to the former garrison town of Huairou. Reportedly, the decision was taken after the Chinese premier, Li Peng, had returned from the UN social summit in Copenhagen, where he was barracked by human rights protesters. He did not want a 'feminist Woodstock' on his doorstep, it was said.

Then, just days before the conference opening, there was the last-minute release of the human rights activist, Dr Harry Wu, amid fears that his detention might jeopardise attendance at the official conference by the USA first lady, Hillary Rodham Clinton. There was confirmation that nuclear testing had been carried out in defiance of world opinion at a time when France was also being condemned. 'China stands for the complete prohibition and thorough destruction of nuclear weapons,' the Chinese foreign minister, Chen Jian, said. 'Possession of a small number of nuclear weapons is solely for the purpose of self-defence.'

There were other reasons for many women to stay away: reports of a recent spate of executions in advance of the conference; visa problems; money problems; and the Thirtieth anniversary of Tibet's designation as an autonomous region. In Ireland, Noreen Byrne, the chairwoman of the National Women's Council (NWC) - the body charged with co-ordinating Irish NGO participation in Beijing - confirmed that she would not travel to China because of her views on the population policy. The Minister of State for Foreign Affairs, Joan Burton, had similar reservations - though not publicly stated. The Irish president, Mary Robinson, found that her attendance would have a price tag - a state visit to China - and did not take the Beijing plane.

Yet Irish women should not allow China's record on human rights and population to deter them from participating, a preparatory conference hosted by the NWC was told in July. To do so would be to

19

fall for 'anti-Chinese propaganda', Amrit Wilson, lecturer in women's studies at the University of Luton, said. Violations of civil liberty were occurring all over the world, not just in China, she reminded her audience.

Like Ireland, India had experienced the worst affects of British colonialism; Amrit's own grandmother's life had been one of poverty and oppression. Similar policies were being pursued by the British government, through its membership of Bretton Woods institutions like the World Bank and the International Monetary Fund - organisations of which Ireland was also a member. Asian women sought support from Irish women for their struggle. 'Don't come to us with your charity and sympathy,' she warned.

Within a week of the conference opening, a study published by one of the UN's own constituents would put the debate into perspective. Socialism had been good for the women of the world, including those of China, the 1995 Human Development Report by the UN Development Programme (UNDP) stated. Under Mao Zedong there had been some significant improvements in women's status after thousands of years of feudalism and oppression. Chinese women's literacy rates had more than doubled in the past fifty years to seventy per cent in 1992, and their enrolment in third-level education had increased tenfold.

The fact that twelve developing countries were able to raise female literacy by more than thirty percentage points between 1970 and 1990 indicated that income was not necessarily a decisive factor. With scarce resources, yet strong political commitment, China, Sri Lanka and Zimbabwe had managed to raise adult women's literacy rates by seventy per cent or more. Several richer countries had lagged behind, such as Gabon and Saudi Arabia, at forty-six per cent and forty-eight per cent respectively.

Still, there was trouble on the horizon. Gains made in socialist countries were now being undermined by the transition to market-oriented economies, the report said. No more so than in China, where many women who had grown up with fair job and schooling opportunities were finding themselves under pressure, in a changing economy, to stay at home. Female infanticide showed no signs of abating, as old biases against women began to emerge again.

No country could afford to congratulate itself upon reading the UNDP text. Unprecedented progress contrasted sharply with unspeakable misery, the report found. Of the estimated 1.3 billion people living in poverty, seventy per cent were female, and access to independent income continued to be a 'distant goal'. Even at global level, women's achievements went unrecognised; since its inception in 1901, only twenty-eight women - including two from Northern Ireland - had received the Nobel prize.

There were other judgments, delivered with considerable force. One woman in six has been raped in her lifetime, according to studies the

UNDP referred to in Canada, New Zealand, Britain and the USA. A third of women have reported sexual abuse during childhood or adolescence. Despite documented rape and torture in recent conflicts, mass violence against women as a weapon of war has not yet been classified as a war crime - a situation which the Beijing conference was to address. And some ninety states had not yet signed or ratified the UN convention on elimination of all forms of discrimination against women (CEDAW) - Ireland being one of forty-three states which had ratified it with reservation.

Women work some thirteen per cent more than men, the report found. Two-thirds of that work is unpaid, compared to only one-fourth to one-third of men's. The workday in rural areas is twenty per cent longer than in urban areas, and worktime in industrial countries is twenty per cent less than in developing countries. Women suffer much more than men from the effects of environmental degradation; and less than ten per cent of bank credit is extended to female clients.

Only Denmark, Finland, Holland, Norway, the Seychelles and Sweden had crossed the thirty per cent threshold for women's representation in parliament and cabinet, with Ireland standing at 12.4 per cent. Not surprisingly, the four Nordic countries - Sweden, Finland, Norway and Denmark - scored highest in terms of gender equality. Yet half a million women worldwide still died every year from pregnancy-related causes. And $11 trillion are 'unaccounted for', currently, in the world economy, because so much of women's work is underpaid, or not rewarded at all. Poverty still wore a distinctly female face.

A 362-paragraph document, known as the Beijing Draft Platform for Action, was intended to address all this in autumn, 1995. Drawn up months before and negotiated by diplomats at preparatory conferences, the document represented the gains of previous women's world conferences, beginning with Mexico in 1975, and continuing in Copenhagen (1980) and Nairobi (1985). 'Rio, Vienna, Cairo, Copenhagen all rolled into one,' was how one Irish NGO delegate, Pauline Eccles of the Irish Commission for Justice and Peace, described other parts of the provisional text which built on agreements made by UN member states at more recent conclaves: the 1992 Earth Summit, the 1993 Human Rights conference, the 1994 Population and Development Conference in Cairo and the 1995 Social Summit in Denmark.

In spite of local sensitivities, human rights formed an integral part of the Platform's agenda, along with poverty, education, health, violence, armed conflict, economic structures and policies, power and decision-making, advancement of women, media, environment and, at the request of the African countries, the situation of the girl child. Within a month of the Beijing conclave, some forty per cent of the draft text was still 'bracketed' - that is, the subject of disagreement among member states. As a wicked August deadline approached, there was a breakthrough on the use of the word 'gender'. Much of the debate would be about such semantics; the use of 'equity' versus 'equality', and 'universal' versus 'universally-recognised' human rights. Fundamentalist states like Iran and Sudan wished to substitute the word 'equity' in the text for 'equality', believing it to give more flexibility in interpretations of inheritance, divorce and employment laws. The outstanding issues would dominate the conference: reproductive rights, over which the Vatican delegation had pledged to do battle after Cairo; third world debt and the effect of structural adjustment policies on women's status and health, representing a link which the USA resisted to the last; and new mechanisms for underpinning resolutions with financial support.

As for the environment, which should also have taken centre stage just three years after Rio, it was given poor billing in spite of the best efforts of NGOs.

An estimated 30,000 registered for the NGO forum - Tibetan and Taiwanese delegates were among those refused entry. Another 17,000 checked in to Beijing's Asian Games village for the largest UN conference on record. Among the ninety-strong delegation from Ireland was Mary McGoldrick, representing Women's Aid.

They arrived in large numbers from all points of the compass, and from very diverse backgrounds. 'Welcome, Sisters from Five Continents!' the banners marking the NGO forum's official opening, complete with silk scarves, blimps, balloons and fireworks, read.

There had been much tension, but little overt security on the day. The city of nineteen million was like a sponge, absorbing the foreign faces with little obvious interest. Yet there were traffic restrictions, special taxis were licensed, and the regular August melon-sellers seemed to have disappeared from the streets. Beijing was reported to be holding its breath for an invasion of 'topless lesbians' - one profile drawn of foreign activists in the Chinese press. In the USA press, a virulent pre-conference propaganda war seemed to have less to do with women's issues and more to do with current Sino-USA relations, strained by the Dr Harry Wu sentencing for spying and rumblings over independence by Taiwan.

'Let's not talk any more about how we got here. We're here,' an exhausted and frustrated executive director of the NGO forum, Irene Santiago, pleaded at a press conference in Huairou. Two days later she would dissolve in tears as journalists continued to bombard her with questions about security, about transport and visa problems, about the China Organising Committee's apparent failure to fulfil its side of the agreement with the UN. The 4,000-strong press was experiencing the worst of times, having been designated special hotels with their own 'protection'. Accommodation had to be paid for, in full, in foreign currency and in advance.

To top it all, it began to rain. No one could remember anything like it. This was not typical Beijing autumn weather. There was a run on umbrellas, and gleeful satellite television reports of women struggling through mud in a boggy, soggy NGO camp out at Huairou.

'Rain will not dampen the spirit of the dancer!' came the clear message from the drum-beating, gong-ringing, song-singing Korean delegation, who had come to the NGO forum to highlight the plight of Asian 'comfort women' subjected to abuse during the second world war. Thousands of other activists were similarly unperturbed, determined to make the most of ten days to raise awareness about poverty, disability, sexual discrimination, health, the environment, violence against women and the effects of a rise in conservative forces within a global world economy.

Aung San Suu Kyi, the recently-released Burmese Nobel Peace Prize winner, would deliver a keynote address by televised link, in which she called for mutual respect between the sexes instead of 'patriarchal domination and degradation'. Education and empowerment of women could not fail to result in a 'more caring, tolerant, just and peaceful life for all', she said. Amnesty International would stage its first demonstration in China, with t-shirts and posters depicting female prisoners of conscience, including Tsultrim Dolma, a Tibetan Buddhist nun.

There would be theatre, music, chat with women the world over by Internet. Irish delegates would travel around Huairou by bike, and delight in simple, ten-dollar-a-day accommodation. And groups like Sisterlove Incorporated, an AIDS prevention group for black women based in Atlanta, Georgia, would hold workshops. In its case, it focused on USA hypocrisy by putting OJ Simpson and the Pope on trial. Pope John Paul II was attempting to row back on agreements made at previous UN conferences, the sisters said. The Vatican, which had participant status at the conference, was 'the only UN member state with zero birth-rate, trying to dictate and control what the population does'.

The USA first lady, Hillary Clinton, President Benazir Bhutto of Pakistan, President Vigdis Finnbogadottir of Iceland, Prime Minister Gro Harlem Brundtland of Norway were among the invited guests to the official conference, which began in Beijing in September, 1995, as the NGO forum drew to a close. Ms Clinton drew ire with a speech critical of China, and that memorable phrase - 'human rights are women's rights and women's rights are human rights, once and for all'. President Bhutto would attempt to explain the position of women within the Muslim religion. Yet the leader of the Vatican delegation, Professor Mary Ann Glendon, threatened to upstage them all.

The Holy See delegation's influence spanned five continents. In contrast to the UN committee charged with implementing the Convention on all Forms of Discrimination against Women (CEDAW), which was given observer status, the Holy See was a full player. Professor Glendon, a fifty-six year old Harvard law professor, did not fit any stereotypes. With a background in civil rights and an interest in new economic approaches to the developing world, she was described as a feminist and a radical, but not a radical feminist; half-Irish, half-American, but not Irish-American; married for the second time but not an advocate of divorce. The European Union,which was awarded status similar to that of the Vatican, was focus for much of Professor Glendon's criticism. The conference's draft document was written in 'strident American dialect', she said. Where was the rich human rights tradition of Europe in all this, she asked, in an interview in Beijing with *The Irish Times*.

And where was the Holy See? Somewhere in there with Islamic states, in an alliance forged at the UN population conference in Cairo. Over a tense week, during which there appeared to be some movement in wording on artificial birth control, including condoms, deep divisions emerged in the wording for the health chapter. After a series of late nights, all references to sexual orientation were dropped and the concept of sexual rights was not included in the summary, or declaration, accompanying the Platform for Action. More than forty countries, mainly Catholic and Islamic, lodged 'reservations' against parts of the text, which was, in any case, non-binding. Significantly, a woman's sexual autonomy was recognised as a human right and rape was recognised as a weapon of war.

Money, as one observer noted, was the only issue to cause as much dissension as sex. The European Union and the USA resisted attempts by the Group of seventy-seven developing countries (G-77) to underwrite commitments made in the Platform. On the positive front, there was victory for the concerted campaign to ensure that women's unpaid work was measured in satellite national accounts, and agreement on continued funding for UN research agencies like UNIFEM and INSTRAW. Significant steps were also taken towards realisation of women's empowerment, access to land and credit and girls' equal right to inheritance.

However, as Mary van Lieshout of Oxfam noted, structural causes of women's poverty were not addressed. Until the international community - led by the USA and European Union - addressed these fundamental injustices in macro-economic policy, eradication of poverty would not be possible, she said in Beijing. As for the environment, the document fudged on making that vital link between economic globalisation, structural adjustment policies and environmental degradation.

NGOs could not be blamed for lack of effort , in spite of attempts by some to accuse 'western imperialist feminists' of dominating the agenda. If anything, seasoned participants like Betty Friedan were borrowing language from 'southern' countries, while the World Bank, which had staged several press conferences to demonstrate its commitment to gender, was speaking with an 'ecofeminist' voice. The loudest message came from organisations like DAWN (Development Alternatives for Women in a New Era), represented by Gita Sen and Devaki Jain; and from guests like Dr Muhammad Yunus, founder of the world famous

Grameen Bank, Bangladesh's 'village' bank.

The challenge, as identified by DAWN, was to counter the negative effects of a current globalising economy, the changing role of the state and the perception that 'growth is good'. A global subterranean economy, based on narcotics, weapons and money-laundering, had influenced the resurgence of global patriarchal forces like religious fundamentalism and cultural nationalism. So, while two sets of 'elites' argued over who had the right to consume and pollute, the health and wealth of women was ignored as a minor issue.

So what was it all about? Long after the final document gathers dust, Beijing may still be remembered as a 'window of opportunity', casting light on that link between local problems and global policies. Such was the conclusion reached by Gretchen Fitzgerald, vice-chair of the Irish Aid Advisory Committee and one of six NGO representatives on the Irish government's official delegation. On her return from China, she identified the lack of financial commitment to additional resources and the failure to agree on internationally-binding legislation which would provide political space for women as the main disappointments.

Nevertheless, 'the unified spirit of women worldwide and the political will, both at NGO and official level, to bring about changes for a less unjust world' characterised the conference for her.

Sure, there were differences over sexual rights, cultural practices. Sure, Sudan's Islamic government pledged that it would not implement any part of a global blueprint on women's lives which conflicted with its interpretation of the Muslim faith. Sure, Saudi Arabia boycotted the conference altogether. Sure, China appeared to agree to everything, in an effort to make sure that their conference was a success; while Chinese activists who were willing critics of their own government were equally strident in defence of the one-child policy.

'Resources, the environment - these are problems that are not even being debated in China yet,' Wu Qing, an outspoken female deputy in the People's Congress and professor of American studies at Beijing Foreign Studies University, told journalists. What was the alternative when China had twenty-two per cent of the world's population on seven per cent of the world's arable land?

'Let us today count our strategic victories, not the tactical defeats,' the Norwegian prime minister, Gro Harlem Brundtland, judged at the closing ceremony. 'What we have achieved is to unbracket the lives of girls and women. Now we must move on ...'

Mary McGoldrick is moving on. Even if she had known what was going to happen to her on the Great Wall, she would still have been there, she says some months later, back in Dublin. Working at a personal, local and, latterly, national level with fellow victims of domestic violence, she found herself in the company of women worldwide in China. She discovered something else: spending so much time with a large group of compatriots, from both sides of the Irish border, she realised that there was much quiet, yet effective, energy being expended on women's issues - relating to poverty, the environment, indigenous groups like the travelling community - at home. A domestic violence bill is due to become law this year in Ireland. There is still a huge 'grey area' not covered by the legislation, in terms of support services, she says. The Irish government made other commitments at the UN conference, which it will be held to. The last twelve months will be seen as a watershed.

'There are a lot of women like me out there,' Mary says. 'They are, or have been, in abusive relationships, and have to be all things to their family: ma, da, counsellor, provider. So I consider myself really lucky to have been out, to see China. It was worth all the pain on the journey back.'

Still in pain, perhaps barely alive, is another woman for whom the Beijing conference offered a life beyond. Slim, slight, carrying four bags and a young child on her arm, Chen Xiao Yue (thirty-four) approached this reporter, and a Canadian colleague, on a Saturday morning in September in Huairou. She had travelled 1,300 kilometres from Jiangsu province, near Shanghai, with her six-year-old daughter, but felt that it would be worth it. A victim of domestic violence, including multiple rape, by her own husband, who wanted a son even if it meant breaking the one-child law, Chen had left home for good when she discovered that her daughter had also been sexually abused.

Handing us an envelope with her testimony, marked by her thumb-print, Chen was hustled away by plain-clothes security. There was a row, tears, screams; we tried to follow; our interpreter was taken for questioning. Chen Xiao Yue had arrived in Huairou a day too late. Most of the NGO conference participants had gone.

We agonised, gave her letter to the hotline run by the Women's Research Institute in Beijing. Driving back to the capital with lumps in our throats, we knew it would have been too easy to report her case as another 'China story'. Chen Xiao Yue could have been a woman in trouble, age immaterial, address *Anywhere* ...

Going Global:
Women and Economic Globalisation

Helen O'Connell

The 1995 Human Development Report tells us that the world today is richer than it was fifty years ago, that from 1950 to 1992 world income increased from US$4 trillion to US$23 trillion.[1] Computers now 'move' more than a trillion dollars around the world's financial markets every twenty-four hours. The last fifty years have brought tremendous advances in medicine and science and unprecedented changes in technology and communications.

In this period too, women in countries have achieved significant recognition and extension of their rights. Very many now can exercise more fully their civil, political, social, economic and cultural rights. Many now have improved access to education and training and control over income and resources. In most countries women are playing increasing roles in decision-making in local and national structures and in political, business and trade union organisations.

These global advances hide some very stark differences within countries and between countries. Within countries there are persistent and widening gaps between women and men, and between different social and ethnic groups. Between countries, north, south, east and west there are sharp contrasts too. Women, men and children living in countries in Africa, Asia, the Pacific, the Caribbean and Latin America - more than three quarters of the world's people - secure only sixteen per cent of the world's income. The richest one-fifth of the world's people enjoy eighty-five per cent of all income.

Despite the advances achieved, women are seventy per cent of the poorest people, twice as many women as men cannot read or write, and girls are sixty per cent of the 130 million children who have no access to primary education. Women produce half of the world's food but own around one per cent of the world's land. The number of rural women living in poverty has increased by fifty per cent in the last twenty years, compared to three per cent for men. Women also represent the highest percentage of the unemployed.

These disturbing inequalities in the production, distribution and enjoyment of wealth are not accidental economic blips. They are the logical and predictable consequences of the dominant model of economic development. The corner stone of this model is economic growth achieved through freeing the market. This market-driven model reached a new level of universality and sophistication in the 1980s and 1990s due to the debt crisis and the economic reform measures promoted by the international financial institutions (International Monetary Fund and World Bank) to deal with it, and the liberalisation and deregulation of trade. The result is an increasing globalisation of services, production and markets.

The debt crisis

A decade of profitable, and uncontrolled lending came to an abrupt halt in 1982 when Mexico threatened to default on its debt repayments. In the 1980s interest rates rose sharply and costs of debt increased accordingly. The world recession, the collapse in commodity prices and increasing restricted access to markets, plus inappropriate debtor government policy decisions made it impossible for debts to be serviced, let alone repaid. The debts spiralled upwards as new loans were borrowed from international financial institutions and Northern governments to cover interest payments on old debts especially those owed to commercial banks. More and more foreign currency was used by indebted governments to pay interest on loans instead of on essential imports like oil or spare parts for industry or in investment in long-term social and economic development. The debt crisis and the measures taken to deal with it have overshadowed most Southern countries ever since. Within a few years the phenomenon of 'reverse flows' had arrived: indebted Southern countries were transferring more in debt servicing to Northern institutions than they were receiving in loans or aid. The net transfer to developing countries fell from US$44 billion in 1980 to minus US$63 billion in 1989. The situation combined with deteriorating trading possibilities to exacerbate and prolong the debt crisis.

The lenders wanted the loans repaid. They insisted that borrowing countries introduce measures to stabilise and adjust their economies, to redress what the lenders called internal and external imbalances. Since the 1980s new lending, and much aid, to developing countries is given under certain conditions defined by the International Monetary Fund and the World Bank. These conditions are packaged as stabilisation and structural adjustment programmes. Without the IMF and World Bank seal of approval - that is, without a stabilisation and structural adjustment programme - indebted countries are deemed ineligible for new credit. Once an indebted country adopts the required economic policy changes, and meets agreed targets, credit becomes available. Increasingly since the mid 1980s much aid is conditional on this seal of approval, as is foreign investment.

The economic reform programmes have one immediate aim: to ensure indebted countries repay the debts and thus sustain the international financial system. A longer-term goal is to integrate developing countries more fully into the free-market global economy.

That indebted Southern countries had to make economic adjustments is irrefutable: their situations were untenable. What is debatable is the nature, scope and duration of these adjustments. Already committed to monetarist economic policies at home, Northern governments and institutions saw little reason why similar policies should not be adopted in the South. The significant differences in economic, social and political realities, North and South, appear to have received little attention; neither did differences between Southern countries. All indebted countries were prescribed the same economic package. The stage of industrial and agricultural development, the extent of poverty and inequality and the nature of colonial legacy were ignored. So too were education and training standards, population size, value of natural resource base, or degree of social cohesion. Countries as poor as Mozambique or Bolivia, or as relatively better-off as Zimbabwe or Chile, were prescribed the same remedy for economic recovery. These differences were to determine the scale of the impact of economic reform on the majority of women, men and children, and ultimately in many countries to undermine any potential long-term benefits of the reform process itself. Even those developing countries, like Bangladesh, with little or no debt, are expected to follow the same economic path if they wish to continue to receive aid and concessional loans.

Stabilise and grow?

Stabilisation programmes are a series of shock measures aimed to achieve a balance of payments equilibrium in a number of years by reducing public and private domestic demand and reducing budgetary deficits. Demand is decreasing principally by devaluing the currency and thereby reducing real incomes, and by removing price controls. Currency devaluation has the added benefit of making exports cheaper and therefore, theoretically at least, more desirable. Budget deficits are lowered by cutting public expenditure, for example, by laying-off public employees, and removing subsidies on basic commodities, such as food or fuel.

The second part of the package, structural adjustment programmes, aimed to bring about economic growth through improving the incentive structure, promoting production for export, liberalising trading relations, deregulating the economy, and privatising state-owned enterprises and public services. The underlying principle of structural adjustment is that the 'market', if freed of government interference and inhibiting regulations, would operate efficiently, ensure economic growth and build a fully-integrated global economy.

Currency devaluation caused sharp falls in real wages, while inflation and the removal of subsidies pushed up the cost of food and other basic commodities. Together with the introduction of charges for health care and education, the result was a dramatic decline in household income and living standards. The cuts in public spending led to reduced public services and job losses, particularly for women for whom that sector had offered good employment opportunities. Industrial workers were also adversely affected as, following trade liberalisation, many domestic industries could not compete with cheaper imports from abroad. Structural adjustment aimed to increase agricultural productivity but ignored the situation of women farmers who generally grow different crops, have limited land rights, restricted access to credit, training and inputs, and often are obliged to provide free labour on their husband's fields.

The debt crisis and the subsequent economic reform process have put enormous strains on women's resources, energy, time and good will. The immediate price women pay is increased poverty, longer hours spent trying to earn some income, and exhaustion. The concept and implementation of structural adjustment programmes are premised on the existing unequal division of rights, roles and responsibilities between women and men. Far from addressing these inequalities, the programmes perpetuate and exacerbate them. Structural adjustment presumes the continuation and extension of women's unwaged work in the home, community and economy. Most women will not turn their back on hungry children in need of food, an ill child in need of moral support. The cost too is opportunities for equality postponed, and in effect, rights rescinded. Women cannot achieve equality in a situation of mounting poverty and insecurity, or when day-to-day survival takes precedence over all else. Structural adjustment programmes decimate the public infrastructure necessary for women to fulfil those family and community responsibilities allocated to them, and at the same time, remove, or severely restrict, the means by which women can attain their equality, namely, education, training, employment and time to organise.

While the present situation of millions of adult women in many countries in Africa, Asia and Latin America is dire, the long-term implications for young girls and women are also daunting: the privatisation of education and the introduction of school fees has meant that many families are forced to choose which of their children to educate. Regrettably, but understandably in some societies, many parents opt to educate their sons. There are other factors too which operate against girls' education: girls are frequently removed from schooling to look after younger siblings while adult family members are out seeking income.

The education of boys and young men is not guaranteed either: in the poorest households, all children are themselves involved in trying to earn some income as street traders, or in other forms of child labour. In the poorest parts of the poorest countries schools no longer function in any normal fashion: educational materials are scarce or non-existent, and teachers are forced to seek additional sources of income to supplement their meagre salaries.

Mozambique provides a stark illustration. Primary school enrolment rates fell from forty-seven to forty per cent from 1987 to 1990 under the Economic Rehabilitation Programme (PRE), Mozambique's structural adjustment programme. Under the PRE, state expenditure on education fell from seventeen per cent to the state budget in 1986 to ten per cent in 1988.[2] Classes reached sizes of sixty to eighty pupils compared with the average of forty-one for Sub-Saharan Africa as a whole.[3] Writing in 1991, Reginald Green reported that many primary schools were operating a two or three shift system, which is exhausting for teachers and limits each child's education to as little as three hours per day.[4]

On narrow economic grounds alone, structural adjustment programmes are flawed. If many indebted countries embark simultaneously on the path of production for export, whether in food crops, manufactured goods or services, the price of these goods or services on the global market will fall correspondingly. Secondly, not all African, Asian or Latin American industries are strong enough to compete effectively in global markets. Thirdly, while the liberalisation of trading relations may assist exports, it has the effect also of making imports cheaper. Added to this, in very many developing countries, the private and public domestic demand for goods and services is so low that local industries cannot sell their products in such sufficient quantities to remain viable. Policies and measures previously regarded as within the remit of individual governments, such as protection of infant industries, subsidies on basic foods, or levels of public sector spending now come under the scrutiny, if not direct ambit, of the World Bank and the IMF. But as Colin Stoneman (1993) and others have pointed out, these very policies of protection and subsidisation were instrumental in bringing about the economic success of countries like Germany and the newly-industrialising countries (NICs), like Brazil.[5]

From the perspective of the lenders, the measures promoted to deal with the debt crisis have succeeded in ensuring indebted countries continue to service the debts. But the strategy has failed to resolve the crisis. The total value of outstanding loans, including grants and loans from Northern governments, the World Bank and the IMF, continues to grow and stood at almost US$2 trillion in 1994; this presents a seven per cent increase on 1993 figures. Each year African governments pay over US$13 billion to Northern creditors, more than double their expenditure on health and primary education.

In human terms, the economic reform process has failed to improve the economic or social well-being of millions of women, men and children in developing countries. There is little evidence that the policy has created the conditions for sustainable economic development in any country. While the debate on whether increased poverty can or cannot be attributed directly to structural adjustment will continue for many decades, what is incontrovertible is that poverty has increased for the majority of women, men and children in the poorest countries, and increased disproportionately for women.

Liberalising trade

Physical barriers to trade, such as tariffs, quotas and regulations are anathema to a global market. Expanding world trade and markets require liberalised trading arrangements and few rules and regulations; liberalisation and deregulating are key planks of the economic reform programmes installed by developing countries. Parallel to this were changes at the international level brought about through the General Agreement of Tariffs and Trade round of talks and final GATT IV agreement in 1993. Average world tariffs were progressively reduced from forty per cent in the late 1940s to five per cent by the end of the GATT round. GATT IV established the World Trade Organisation to undertake the supervision of world trade. Its remit is wider than GATT and it has greater means of enforcing agreements. It relates directly to the World Bank and the IMF.

Under the final GATT agreement, in writing at least, all countries have equal access to international markets. Countries in Asia, the Pacific, the Caribbean, Latin America and Africa hoped for far greater access to the rich markets of Europe, North America and elsewhere but, in practice, their access to the rich markets of Europe, North America and elsewhere but, in practice, their access remains quite limited. Non-tariff restrictions are still widely used and it is always possible to restrict imports by using such grounds as quality standards.

In the years 1965 to 1990 world trade in merchandise tripled and trade in services increased more than fourteenfold.[6] While most trade is between industrialised countries, the amount of trade between developing and industrialised countries has increased too. Increasingly over the last fifteen to twenty years most Southern countries are involved in international trade and overall their share of world manufacturing exports have grown from five to twenty-five per cent. It is estimated that by the year 2000, around ninety per cent of the world's people will live in countries strongly connected to the world market. The overall picture, however, hides some sharp regional variations. Many countries in East and South Asia and Latin America have been able to export and import more. South East Asia, in particular, accounts for three quarters of developing countries' share of world manufacturing exports. Most African countries are in a much weaker position. Due to global economic changes, they have lost much of their previous economic strengths in exporting raw materials, such as copper, and traditional commodities, like cotton or coffee.

While extolling the virtues of 'free-trade' abroad, industrialised countries have established new trading blocks at home, such as the European Union and the North America Free Trade Agreement, to protect their regional interests. There are conflicting views on whether these blocks undermine or advance progress towards global free trade. For me there is a more fundamental question: can developing countries participate as equal members in the global economy where seventy per cent of trade is between and within transnational corporations (and forty per cent is controlled by 350 companies), and where trading structures are firmly biased in favour of the big players?

As world markets have expanded, transnational corporations (TNCs) have grown in scope, power and influence. Developments in new technology, telecommunications and transportation changed the face of economic operations from the 1960s. Companies from North America, Europe, Japan and elsewhere relocated the labour-intensive parts of their production to Southern countries. They were keen to avoid the high wages demanded at home due to near full employment and were enticed by the financial incentives, cheaper labour, few regulations and non-union agreements offered by developing country governments eager to attract foreign investment. Most companies relocated to produce cheaply for export, some to produce for local consumption. Accounting and administrative functions were relocated abroad also as advances in technology and telecommunications allowed. The service industry quickly followed manufacturing and sited its labour-intensive operations, such as data processing, in Southern countries. Trade in services is now the fastest growing element in world trade; it includes finance and insurance, tourism, shipping and telecommunications. Trade in services now accounts for approximately twenty per cent of the total and around forty per cent of the value of exports in manufacturing goods.[7]

Transnational corporations and international finance companies together dominate the global economy. Global trade, finance and credit, transportation and intellectual property rights are all within their domain and for the most part outside the jurisdiction of governments. TNCs, alone, control one-third of global private sector productive assets. Their position is not always obvious as they operate through complicated systems of licensing and sub-contracting.

The facts and figures about world trade hide important details, ever widening gaps in access to wealth, employment and productive resources. The poorest one-fifth of the world's people control one per cent of world trade.

International division of labour

Economic globalisation brings with it a very sophisticated international division of labour within which women workers have a particular place ordained by gender, race and class. Women, and young women in particular, are the preferred workers for relocated labour-intensive production and services. In production and assembly line work in South East Asia, for example, young women comprise eighty to ninety per cent of the workforce. One recent study showed that women data processors in the Philippines earned twelve-times less than women doing the same work in the UK. Companies want a workforce which is cheaper than at home, which is willing to work long hours carrying out tedious and repetitive tasks often in hazardous conditions, is reliable, obedient and not too ambitious. The stereotype of the 'docile and nimble-fingered' young Asian woman worker is being debunked as evidence of women workers' organising actions mounts, but is still used by some Asian governments anxious to attract foreign investment. For their part, company managers go to great lengths to regiment the workplace and suppress workplace organisation. The threat that they will close down and move elsewhere is used frequently by companies to discourage demands for better conditions.

Jobs in export-oriented production or services enable women to earn income and develop an identity for themselves outside their home and family circle. The income they earn, which is usually higher than they could earn elsewhere, is vital to the wellbeing of their families. The other side of the story is that these jobs are very few relative to the number of women seeking employment, confine women workers within rigidly sex-segregated and labour-intensive occupations, and are ultimately precarious. As Chant and McIlwaine (1994) point out, global demands for products, economic upturns or downturns, company restructuring or enhanced profitably elsewhere all determine how long companies remain in any one location and thus the stability of women's employment.[8]

More generally, the push to export-oriented production or services has decided limitations as a long-term development strategy. While the contribution to export figures is important, in most cases, the hoped-for technology transfer and stimulus to economic development outside the special processing zones have not materialised. The number of jobs is low and little training is provided. Senior management positions are few and frequently held by non-nationals.

Unemployment is rising worldwide. At the end of 1995 there were around twenty million women and men without waged work in the European Union. The 1995 Human Development Report estimates that one billion new jobs are needed in developing countries in the next decade.[9] It is not clear from where these jobs will come as the prevailing view is that to increase productivity companies must introduce more technology and job cuts. The phenomenon of jobless growth has emerged: increased world income accompanied by decreased wealth distribution. A small elite acquire great wealth or have well paid jobs, the majority earn a little, and a significant percentage are surplus to the needs of the global economy. Women are disproportionately in the latter two categories. There is a mushrooming in casual and part-time employment and in homeworking and, of course, many of these jobs are low paid and done by women. Workers are told they must be flexible to survive. Small scale enterprises are squeezed out, or forced into, the global economy. They are dependent on inputs - whether technology, consumer goods or raw materials - the source of which is increasingly within the dominion of the global market.

For millions of women and men the informal sector is their only economic opportunity and this sector is growing in almost all countries. More and more women and men crowd into the informal economy to become street traders, taxi-drivers, collectors of waste paper and bottles for recycling, car windscreen washers, domestic workers, or drug dealers. Traders sell anything they can make or buy. The informal sector has its hierarchy too and women do not compete on an equal footing with men. Women in the Philippines complain that men can start selling earlier in the morning while they are still busy with children and domestic responsibilities. Women in Angola complain of violence from men over key selling sites and bullying from self-appointed market-bosses.

Migration is a growing trend. Moving from rural to urban areas or to another country has become the only survival option, albeit precarious, for millions of women and men. The International Labour Organisation estimates that worldwide there are around 100 million economic migrants and refugees. Migrant workers experience discrimination on many levels, including, for example, different civil and employment rights, contract violations, harassment and violence. It is often the most able and better skilled that migrate thus draining their countries of trained and professional workers. The most widely available jobs for migrants are, however in construction, domestic work and catering. Many women migrants become embroiled in the sex industry in Europe and elsewhere. Many are undocumented workers who without permits and official contracts are doubly vulnerable to manipulation and abuse. Migrant workers make a significant contribution to the economies in which they work and to their home economies in form of remittances. This double subsidy is rarely acknowledged. The remittances sent home by Filipino migrant workers is estimated at US$5 billion. Five billion in 1993 is roughly equivalent to the amount the Filipino government pays annually in debt servicing.

The role of aid
Aid from European and other Northern governments has played its role in fostering globalisation. Commercial considerations have always influenced aid decisions: in the post-colonial period Northern governments were keen to open up markets, gain or retain access to resources and gave aid to further these interests. Now, while the stated objective of the aid or development cooperation of the European Union and its Member States is poverty reduction, the main strategy for achieving this is by integrating developing country economies into the global economy - a global economy which is characterised by widening inequality and poverty.

The aid and development cooperation policy of the European Union and its Member States is by and large still shaped by belief in the 'free-market' economic development model and the IMF/World Bank line on economic reform. Other aid priorities are stated, such as equality between women and men, good governance, respect for human rights and environmental protection and are regarded seriously by many donors, but in practice, economic reform overrides all other policy commitments. In the late 1980s donor governments and institutions began to add political conditions to the existing economic conditions attached to aid. One motivation was that economic reform was not working because many Southern governments were undemocratic, unaccountable, and lacking in transparency and competence. The political conditions included democracy, good governance, and respect for human rights - an impressive agenda and one which aid could greatly advance. There is little evidence, yet, that aid donors are allocating significant resources in this direction. Furthermore, there are some fundamental contradictions between the donors' economic and political agendas. The gender dimensions of the political agenda are beginning to receive some donor attention now.

Signs of hope

In the last twenty years women's organisations and networks have flourished alongside other broad social movements. They are working for social, economic and political change throughout the South and North. They are working, often against impossible obstacles, for day-to-day survival, and to challenge the structures which exploit and marginalise the majority of people. Women's organisations are taking the lead in uncovering inequalities and putting them on the political agenda.

Over the last ten years more and more voices have questioned the sustainability of the dominant economic model. People's protest movements are gaining influence and demanding policy changes; the opposition to the Narmada Dam in India is the best known recent example but there are hundreds of other actions, local, national and international. Thinking on alternative development models is gaining ground and respectability even in official circles. Feminist economists are exposing the gender-bias in orthodox economic theory and questioning the myths that markets are free, economics are gender-neutral and only work which is waged is economically productive.

The Platform for Action agreed at the UN Fourth World Conference on Women in Beijing in September 1995 contained many progressive recommendations. One of importance here is the agreement to count and value unwaged work. The 1995 Human Development Report estimated that US$16 trillion of global output is 'invisible' because it is unwaged or underwaged. US$11 trillion of this work is done by women.[10] Putting a monetary value on unwaged work for national accounting purposes gives this work visibility and economic status. It is an important step towards ensuring women's social and economic policy interests are recognised and satisfied.

The Social Chapter of the Maastricht Treaty and European Commission directives on social affairs provide the basis for a better balance between economic and social concerns. European Union directives on the rights of part-time workers and on maternity leave, when coupled with the ILO conventions and standards, for example, on employment conditions or on workers with family responsibilities, provide useful examples of ways in which social and economic life could be organised differently not only in Europe but worldwide.

Recent policy changes at the European level indicate some movement in thinking. The resolution on structural adjustment agreed by the Council of Development Ministers on 1 June 1995 calls for much greater flexibility in design and implementation of economic reform programmes to take into account regional and national situations. It calls for assessment of the implications of economic changes on women and men. If this approach were followed fully in the EU's dealings with developing countries, it could reduce poverty and inequality. Another EU resolution agreed in late December 1995 provides grounds for hope also. The resolution, Integrating Gender Issues in Development Cooperation, is the first EU comprehensive policy statement on gender and development issues. It states that promoting equality between women and men is an inherent and indispensable part of the development process and sets out clear recommendations and a timetable for action. Public interest and pressure will play a key role in transforming these resolutions into action.

On a more general note, there is growing acknowledgement that economic growth alone is insufficient to reduce poverty, and that measures must be taken to ensure some wealth is distributed. The 1995 World Development Report of the World Bank conceded that trade unions did have a role to play in economic life.[11] Some transnational corporations are bowing to the inevitability of environmental regulation.

The shortcomings of the global economy as it is currently structured are many. Firstly, countries in Latin America, Africa, Asia, in the Caribbean and Pacific, and now in Eastern and Central Europe are not free to choose their path to development. Secondly, the whole ethos of the global economy is to maximise and accumulate wealth, and not distribute it. The ethos is short-term. There is an unprecedented mobility of capital which can move finance within seconds, and can avoid economies with good labour or environmental codes. There is a massive monopolisation of resources, wealth and technology, over-consumption by the majority in the North and a minority in the South. Everything, including most aspects of our lives, has become a commodity. Thirdly, the arms trade is enormous and critically important to the economies of the North. This poses a fundamental problem few in power are willing to tackle. Fourthly, poverty is increasing. Around 1.2 billion women, men and children do not have enough to live healthily each day.

It is possible to take immediate action to reduce poverty and advance social and economic equality and justice. It is possible to ensure that those living in extreme poverty get a share of wealth, that those on low wages get a better deal and that those needing state welfare can live with dignity. The means are well within the capacities of the global economy. It is possible to make the global economy more democratic, to make the international financial institutions accountable, and to regulate transnational corporations and international finance. It is possible, and urgent, to take steps to build a different world with greater equality and genuine democracy.

NOTES:
1. UNDP, (1995) Human Development Report 1995. New York and Oxford, Oxford University Press.
2. Correia, J I E et al. (1993) The social dimensions of economic structural adjustment programmes in Southern Africa - with special reference to Mozambique. Paper presented to the Winder School on The social dimensions of economic structural adjustment programmes in Southern Africa: case studies organised by the University of Zimbabwe and the Zimbabwean Institute on Southern Africa, Harare, 4-23 June 1993.
3. World University Service (WUS) (1994). Education in Mozambique: Addressing the Approaching Crisis. London, WUS.
4. Green, Reginald H. (1991) The struggle against absolute poverty in Mozambique, SDA Project, National Directorate of Planning, Republic of Mozambique.
5. Stoneman, Colin. (1993) 'The World Bank: some lessons for South Africa' in Review of African Political Economy, No 58, November 1993, Abingdon UK Carfax Publishers for ROAPE Publications.
6. UNDP, (1995) Human Development Report 1995. New York and Oxford, Oxford University Press.
7. Joekes, Susan. (1995) A gender perspective on development and international trade. Presentation to International Coalition for Development Action (ICDA) Annual Conference, Brussels, October 14, 1995.
8. Chant, Sylvia, and Cathy McIlwaine. (1994) Gender and export manufacturing in the Philippines: continuity or change in female employment? The case of the Mactan Export Processing Zone. Paper prepared for Gender Issues Panel, European Conference on Philippines Studies, School of Oriental and African Studies, University of London, April 13-15 1994.
9. UNDP, (1995) Human Development Report 1995. New York and Oxford, Oxford University Press.
10. UNDP, (1995) Human Development Report 1995. New York and Oxford, Oxford University Press.
11. World Bank, (1995) World Development Report. Washington. World Bank.

Trade Liberalisation in Chile:
Women in Crisis

Siobhán Creaton

Chile: A Country of Dramatic Contrasts

Since Chile shook off the shackles of dictatorship five years ago, the economy has gone from strength to strength. But for the many mothers forced to put in long hours of dangerous work for little pay, Chile's economic miracle owes much to its reliance on cheap labour and exploitation of women. There is no denying the country's achievement in macro-economic terms. Its export sector is booming, official unemployment rates are low, and the average per capita income is estimated to be around $2,500 to $2,700.[1]

Now well on its way to joining the North American Free Trade Agreement (NAFTA), this prosperous, vibrant economy is said to be putting its Latin American neighbours to shame. Growing at a rate of more than six per cent a year, Chile has become the role model for its neighbouring states. An economic miracle - or is it?

Within twenty-four hours of arriving in Santiago it became clear to me that Chile is more remarkable for its extremes of poverty and wealth. The statistics are of course accurate. Chile is a thriving economy. However, many of its 13.9 million men, women, and children have yet to share the spoils.

The Other Chile

In the mid 1970s, Chile had begun a process of economic structural change which has had a profound effect. Abandoning policies designed to protect native industries, the government reduced its presence in the productive sectors of the economy and embraced the principles of free trade with a view to fostering prosperity. Characterised by an opening up to foreign trade through the reduction of tariffs and custom duties, and the adoption of anti-inflationary policies, the then military government virtually eliminated all price controls and introduced radical reforms to promote strong economic growth. Its success today is a testament to these policies, which are still rigidly adhered to some twenty years on.

On paper, Chile hasn't put a foot wrong in terms of economic management. Looking beyond the figures, however, it soon becomes apparent that much of Chile's wealth has been amassed through a heavy dependence on cheap, casual labour, and the proliferation of labour laws that deny workers rights. I was repeatedly told that 'there are two

Chiles'.

On a cold night, deep in the Aconcagua Valley, I met a group of around twenty people who revealed the other side of Chile. The journey, through the endless slums that characterise the outskirts of Santiago, did little to prepare me for what lay ahead. Nightfall, I knew, had hidden much of the physical deprivation. Its sheer scale and impact, however, was etched on the lives of the fruit workers I met there. A hut of timber loosely held together with a few nails passed for the local community hall. I was lucky, they said; now at least they had a light bulb to illuminate the proceedings.

Travelling to this 'community centre' mostly by foot, the group, many of them cradling sleeping children, recounted their side of the story. The group works for up to four months every season for local companies, harvesting and packaging kiwis and grapes for export. There is no other work available here. Gloria is one of almost a million seasonal fruit workers in Chile. Married with three children, she has been doing this type of work for as long as she can remember. During the four month season, Gloria often puts in a sixteen-hour day, seven days a week. At the end of the month she usually manages to take home close to $200 (£123.50). Most of the day is spent standing, broken only by a ten minute break for tea and bread in the evening. 'We are not treated as human beings', she explains, but is clearly too tired and weary to register a strong protest. To go to work, Gloria has to leave her children, aged between two and eight years, at home alone. They, like neighbouring children, are forced to fend for themselves. Constantly concerned for their safety and well-being during her long absences, Gloria admits it is difficult to cope. She uses her earnings to clear the slate at the local shops to ensure that her family is offered credit again this year.

Reluctantly joining the conversation, her colleagues tell similar tales. Carmita, a young woman in her early twenties, is in poor health and has been told that she will soon be unable to work. Her doctor has reluctantly warned her that the best she can hope for is to be able to work for another two years in her current job. Suffering from persistent skin complaints and kidney infections, her illnesses, which are common to seasonal workers, are believed to be linked to constant exposure to pesticides.

Working in fields while overhead planes spray the crops with a cocktail of chemicals, the women are in little doubt that the pesticides are taking their toll on their health. Their children are also suffering. For many years now there has been a very high incidence of infant abnormalities in the area and many of the local children have suffered mild cases of poisoning, because the water supply has been contaminated.

Despite their obvious concerns and persistent ill health, the women admit they have done little to protest about their working conditions. 'You become resigned when you see little possibility that anything will change. We just put up with it,' Carmita says. She recalls one worker who raised her recurrent illnesses with their boss, suggesting the pesticides were unsafe. He calmly told her she was suffering from 'nerves' and fired her.

'There is too much at stake to risk complaining' remarks Gloria. With a smile the women say they 'keep the faith', searching for a glimmer of hope in the cruel winter night.

Further meetings with workers in Chile's booming fishing, manufacturing and forestry sectors, highlighted similar abuse and destitution amongst its workforce. Some thirty per cent of the workforce in the fishing industry work onshore in the fish processing plants, where health and safety conditions are precarious. Some of the fish factories have progressed to providing protective clothing, although much of it is rendered useless because of its poor quality.

One of the state's most important fishing centres is found in Talcahuano, a port beside Chile's second city, Concepcion. One of the main employers is the fishing business, Empresa Pesquera San Jose. Almost eighty per cent of the workers at its canning factory are women. All are employed on a casual basis for up to six months of the year. Again the hours worked in the fishing sector are well above the statutory limit of a forty-eight hour week and no more than ten hours a day.

Monica, for instance, explains that she never knows what time she will be able finish work. Typically she works for twelve hours a day, but her shift often drags on for longer periods at the height of the season. Monica's job is to pack the cans of processed fish into boxes as they come off the production line for which she is paid an average of $200 per month. The long shifts are taking their toll, however, and she complains of pains in her arms. Working conditions in the forestry and mining industries are no better.

Competitive Poverty

Chile's thriving export sector depends on a plentiful supply of cheap, casual labour. Low wages, poor conditions and insecurity of work are central to Chile's export success, but these ingredients generate a high level of poverty and stress amongst those in poverty, ie. 'the employed poor'. Lack of commitment to provide full-time jobs - with, for example, pension and social insurance rights - has meant that the fruit, forestry, and fishing industries have been able to hoard profits over the years while the workers are forced to live in poverty.

The minimum wage is 52,150 pesos, or $120 a month, but in reality many Chileans earn a lot less. Almost forty-six per cent of Chilean men and women receive wages that do not cover basic necessities and one third of the population qualifies as indigent or poor.[2]

The wide-scale poverty has forced children as young as fifteen to join the workforce, while the number of women working outside the home is rising rapidly. The most recent statistics show that women make up close to twenty-nine per cent of the workforce, employed mainly in the services sector.[3]

Typically earning up to fifty per cent less than their male

counterparts, even in the top jobs, few women could claim to hold a full-time job, with social insurance provisions and holiday and maternity benefits.

While the number of jobs available for women is growing quickly, they are, according to Estrella Diaz, a director at the Instituto de la Mujer (Women's Institute), largely low-skilled, poorly paid, and offer few opportunities for advancement.

'Contrary to the macro-economic indicators, Chile is very poor' Diaz says. 'There is a great divide between the wealthy and the poor, between men and women. A high proportion of women who work in Chile are single and adolescent mothers. They are very vulnerable and tend to accept poor working conditions' she explains. 'They can't aspire to important jobs so they mainly do manual work, where exploitation is highest. These women have children and won't risk losing their jobs despite the appalling conditions.'

According to Diaz, a lot of women take on 'piece work' - sewing and finishing garments for the clothing industry in their homes at night - or other domestic chores, in addition to their other work. 'Most women work because they have to', she states. 'Few are motivated by personal development.'

Compounding the unstable nature of their employment, most women work where little or no training is provided to help educate them and improve their prospects of gaining better paid employment.

Highlighting the absence of child care services available to working mothers, Diaz says the law also fails to protect their basic rights. Although Chile's antiquated labour law - written in 1980, but archaic in its lack of modern workers' rights - does not endorse discrimination against women, or punish discrimination against women. This makes it considerably easier for such abuses to occur.

At present the government's proposed labour code reforms continue to flounder in the Senate. 'Legally, employers are able to establish more restrictive conditions for access to jobs, career advancement, and salary payment to women' says Diaz. And while the present government has proposed certain changes to the labour code, the likely amendments she expects will make little difference for women.

Despite the large number of women now working in Chile, Diaz claims few are financially better off. The availability of a rising number of poorly paid, insecure jobs, she suggests, has mainly contributed to greater pressures on family life, ailing health and a high degree of drug-abuse.

'Competitive poverty' she calls it, referring to the practice of countries to drive wages and benefits to the lowest common denominator to remain competitive with other countries. Remaining 'competive' - which has led to Chile's export success - has been achieved largely through this reliance on cheap labour and exploitation of women.

Diaz relates how jobs, which were previously permanent with a pension and social insurance entitlements, are now becoming short term and insecure. 'Employers are trying to become more competitive while the workers are paying the price.' She believes that further trade liberalisation, through for example, Chile's accession to NAFTA, will make working conditions equally difficult for men and women in the future. Because women are already in a worse position, she fears their subordination will be reinforced.

Fruit pickers taking a break from work. In the last twenty years, three new export industries have emerged - fishing, forestry and fruit - providing Chile with thirty per cent of its foreign exchange earnings. But the cost in terms of labour force exploitation can be a sixteen-hour day of badly paid, unregulated and insecure work.

Photograph by Julio Etchart.

Trade Liberalisation and Growth

Free trade has undoubtedly helped Chile's major export industries of fruit, fishing, and mining to take off over the past twenty years.

Its biggest export is copper, accounting for more than thirty-seven per cent of its total foreign trade. Fresh and processed fruits make up around ten per cent of Chile's exports, closely followed by wine, forestry and fishmeal products, which are sold in Asia, Europe, neighbouring Latin American states and the USA. Chile is one of the Latin American countries with the least restrictive import measures, with taxes hovering at eleven per cent, and some sanitary measures to protect the fruit industry.

Imports mainly from Asia and the USA have flourished under Chile's relatively free trade policies. Last year, imports of oil and raw materials or semi-manufactured products account for over two thirds of the $10.6 billion of goods imported in 1994.[4]

With a strong history of free trade, Chile naturally aspires to join an international trading alliance such as NAFTA, the pact which liberalises trade between the USA, Canada and Mexico. Recent US Congress decisions may, however, considerably postpone its accession to this union, which aims to establish a European-style market, with a population of 370 million and a combined output of about $7 trillion.

Another major trade alliance which Chile is considering is one with Mercosur, an affiliation based around manufacturing agreements between Argentina, Brazil, Uraguay, and Paraguay. Chile has not yet joined Mercosur but is negotiating some form of bilateral agreement.

Chile is also a member of the Asian and Pacific Economic Cooperation (APEC) group which brings together the countries of the Pacific Rim and has signed an array of bi-lateral agreements with Mexico, Argentina, Venezuela, Bolivia, and Columbia. The government has also indicated that it hopes to conclude a trade agreement with the European Union.

These agreements reflect Chile's heavy dependence on trade. Exports and imports combined account for almost half of the state's gross national output. For over twenty years its liberal policies have supported a thriving import and export sector which has contributed handsomely to its enormous wealth today.

The rising number of outlets for its goods has generated jobs in the Chilean economy since the 1970s. Officially, unemployment now stands at around six per cent - levels much envied by European states, but these figures mask high levels of underemployment. The new jobs, which have brought a substantial number of women into the workforce over the years, are precarious, insecure, low-skilled, and badly paid. 'Liberalisation has allowed more women to go into the workforce, and while this appears to be a big advancement - in statistical terms - most of the jobs are low quality and low skilled', according to Diaz.

Free trade, she says, doesn't improve women's predicament but 'maintains their position of subordination'. She stresses however that it is not just poor women who are suffering the effects of free trade. 'Middle-class women working in banks and other financial institutions are feeling its impact. In a move towards improving the competitiveness of the sector, they are finding their work being contracted out. It is now common practice of banks, for instance, to contract out all of their secretarial and administrative services to reduce their own costs.'

Through greater liberalisation of trade under NAFTA, the import sector is forecast to grow strongly, with goods, often cheaper, and higher quality which are predicted to flood the market, putting many jobs at risk.

Traditional industries, such as the textile, leather, and footwear sectors are expected to bear the brunt of the pain. Corrie and Tamara, two of seven workers at a small textile co-operative operating in a poor marginal neighbourhood in the outskirts of Santiago, are fearful for their livelihood.

For almost twenty years, the small workshop at the back of Corrie's house has been a hive of activity, producing clothes for men, women, and children which are sold in the local markets. The proceeds of a family bequest offered Corrie and her family an independent livelihood that has provided a small but comfortable home in their poor neighbourhood.

Corrie says that while the family has managed to build up a healthy business over the years, it is now facing an increasingly uncertain future. 'While I am not usually pessimistic, I have to admit that our future looks black.'

In the past couple of years their business has been badly affected by cheaper imports from Taiwan, Korea, and other Asian countries, many of which cost up to fifty per cent of their range. Many of the large department stores, she says, are also buying huge stocks of imported clothes, selling them off at knock-down prices that they are unable to match.

'Last year we could maintain a level of sales, and while we didn't make a large profit, we were able to hold on. But this year it's worse,' says Corrie. 'If this continues we may be forced to start buying cheaper imports to sell in the markets ourselves but we can't even imagine things coming to that.' The thought of further liberalisation of trade under NAFTA, she says, is 'frightening'.

Official opinion stresses that Chile has already been a relatively open economy for the best part of twenty years, and takes the view that further liberalisation can only enhance its prosperity.

This line is vigorously upheld in all forms of general public information, something which Non-Govermental Organisations (NGOs) such as Oxfam find frustrating: 'Information on NAFTA and other free trade agreements has always been scarce and biased in favour of the benefits for Chile. Official newsletters studiously avoid references to any likely adverse effects,' says Mary Sue Smiaroski of Oxfam in Chile.

Trade Unions

Union membership was effectively outlawed in the first phase of the military dictatorship, and the unions' national congress, federations, and confederations had their assets seized.

During the late seventies, labour law was amended to allow a very restricted form of union organising. The transition to democracy under Patricio Aylwyn in 1989 brought labour reforms which got rid of some of the worst aspects of Pinochet laws, although they clearly do not protect workers adequately.

According to Pablo Saball, a senior official at the Territorio, an NGO charged with developing labour legislation, the current proliferation of contract-type or casual work in many sectors of the economy has served to suppress the formation of trade unions. Today fewer than twelve per cent of the Chilean workforce is unionised. Saball predicts that things will get even worse for women workers in the future in the absence of strong organisations to lobby for better conditions.

In the fruit industry, fewer than three per cent of all workers are members of a union. One of the reasons for this is that under Chilean law, a union cannot be formed unless there are fifteen or more permanent employees on the payroll. The vast majority of these workers are however seasonal and temporary workers.

Organising seasonal workers into a union has proved to be a vast problem, especially as many roam around the country in search of work. And it is these workers who are most vulnerable to exploitation.

Union organisation is at a more advanced stage of development in the fishing industry though, where in some areas a number of fish processing plants have union representation and a high proportion of women members. Typically up to twenty-six per cent of fisheries workers will be in a union.

Instituto de Capacitacion y Apoyo Rural (ICAR), the training and rural support unit, supported by Oxfam, believes that workers will only secure improved working and living conditions by orchestrating their demands through workers' organisations. Through a programme of training advice for temporary agricultural workers, particularly women, ICAR claims to be making modest progress. Groups like ICAR believe that the accession to NAFTA will ultimately destroy many sectors of the economy. Traditional industries such as agriculture, textiles, clothing, leather, and footwear will immediately come under threat from cheaper imports, signalling wide-scale job losses and further deprivation. And, while admitting that greater access to international markets will certainly accrue to the wineries and the producers of fruit and frozen food, they hold out little prospect that the workers in these thriving sectors, particularly women, will be better off.

ICAR's main concerns centre on the government's failure to adopt a development plan to coincide with the move towards greater liberalisation of trade. 'The economy will be forced to respond to market forces with no controls in place for workers in vulnerable sectors.'

Historically, ICAR claims that structural changes within the economy have always tended to affect women more than men. 'Free trade is a frightening prospect for women. Many will lose their jobs as traditional industries come under threat. In other sectors it is largely women who will be forced to endure further hardship under free trade,' according to ICAR. 'The government is not handling the problems that free trade is likely to throw up for women,' it claims, 'it has been silent.'

One of ICAR's project directors, Coca, who works primarily with workers in the agriculture and fruit sectors, says the fruit export sector has already undergone many changes as part of the process of modernisation in preparation for NAFTA. These changes, she says, are having an enormous effect on workers.

'For women, the transition towards greater competition has led to dramatic changes in their work practices and their family lives,' Coca says. 'Women's self-esteem has risen as they contribute to household income and has left them less dependent on men. This has also acted to improve relationships between women who are now regularly meeting in the workplace. But at the same time, the levels of exploitation in their domestic situation and in work is on the increase.'

Coca explains: 'They see that their new roles haven't made them any better off. They are still in poverty, the quality of their lives has diminished.'

Trade unions, while valued by women, have very little to offer them, she feels. The unions have been slow to adopt new themes and to reflect women's issues, she says. 'In a sense, women feel marginalised as the unions continue to ignore their struggle.'

To join a union is also a big risk for many workers. Many members immediately become part of a 'blacklist', circulated among employers making it impossible to get another job. 'You can't blame competition for everything,' Coca stresses. 'Labour law doesn't favour workers either. These workers don't have a history of unions and are therefore unaware of what can be achieved.'

Pablo Saball believes that the greatest problem facing women in Chile is the blatant disrespect for the law. NAFTA or other free trade agreements, he says are only part of the problem: 'It is the lack of respect, lack of enforcement of labour laws, and the consequent perpetration of exploitation that represents the greatest threat to women's rights,' claims Saball.

There Are Two Chiles
There are two Chiles. There is the thriving vibrant economy - a miracle - which has become the envy of many developing nations. But the poverty, exploitation, stress, and sickness which afflict many of Chile's four million poor people cannot be ignored.

It is arguable that the success of Chile's free trade policies over the years owes much to the millions of workers who have endured great hardship in the spirit of competition. In moving closer to further liberalisation, the Frei government, democratically elected in 1994, must honor its commitment to develop and resource social programmes and combat poverty.

Employers must be made to respect laws. Tougher environmental controls and the adoption of legislation to protect women and children are a priority. The critical question for Chile, and other developing nations pursuing export lead growth strategies, is whether equity and poverty reduction can be achieved while such strategies dominate economic policy.

NOTES:
1. World Bank, (1995), *World Development Report*, Washington, World Bank.
2. CEPAL, (UN Commission for Latin America and the Caribbean), 1993.
3. UNDP, (1995), *Human Development Report: 1995*, New York, Open University Press, 1995.
4. Central Bank of Chile, 1994.

Focus on

'Flexibility' in Chile

Ruth Mayne

Chile's export 'success', which is now seen as a model for the rest of the region, has been based on the idea of deregulating labour markets. Labour reforms introduced under Pinochet were enforced by repression and involving a severe erosion of workers' rights (collective bargaining, the right to strike, and protection from unfair dismissal), as well as of labour standards relating to work contracts and social security benefits. This contributed to the rise in the number of people living in poverty from twenty per cent of the population in 1970, to forty per cent in 1990; whilst the richest twenty per cent of households increased their share of total consumption from forty-five per cent in 1960 to sixty per cent in 1989.

Recent changes in labour law have not adequately improved worker's rights. 'Flexibility' remains a central element of the government's growth with equity strategy. Although the new reforms grant full-time employees greater possibility for collective bargaining, continued restrictions on the right to strike means employers have the right to contract new workers immediately if wage offers consistent with the rise in inflation are turned down. 'Flexible' workers who are subcontracted to work from home, or who have temporary or short-term contracts, are still excluded from the possibility of collective bargaining. This includes fruit, fishing, and forestry workers.

The result of this deregulation has been the spread of 'flexible' working conditions across the economy. Growing numbers of workers in the formal sector are employed on a part-time or casual basis. According to official figures, fourteen per cent of the salaried workers in 1990 did not have a contract; independent estimates put the figure at around thirty per cent in the fruit exporting sector.[1]

There has also been a growth in sub-contracting to home piece-workers, and to family or informal businesses; twelve per cent of employees work from home, twenty-one per cent work in the informal sector, and twenty-one per cent in micro-enterprises. Nearly forty per cent of workers are not covered by pension schemes, a proportion which has increased since 1990.[2]

In Recoleta, Santiago, Oxfam supports a women's training programme with some 12,000 non-unionised women who work in garment workshops. Few of the six thousand workshops meet the specifications of current labour laws; most of the women have no contracts, health or retirement insurance; their safety is compromised by piles of material and merchandise towering over them; camera surveillance of the shop floor is common, and talking with co-workers is forbidden.

Measures to improve salaries and conditions to improve conditions of workers are urgently needed. These measures should include appropriate regulation of the new flexible labour markets, ensuring adequate protection and social insurance for part-time, temporary, and home-workers.

Social regulation of trade and investment agreements is needed to protect workers' basic rights in line with ILO conventions and help reverse the trend towards low-wage export strategies and the dismantling of labour standards.

SOURCE: *Economic Reform and Inequality in Latin America* by Ruth Mayne, Oxford: Oxfam, 1995.

NOTES:
1. Leiva F and Agacino R (1994), 'Flexible Labour Markets, Poverty and Social Disintegration in Chile'.
2. *ibid*

Seventy-two hours in a day? ... With government cutbacks in health spending, women such as volunteer health worker Florence Muhindo compensate for the deteriorating public health services with their own time and labour. (Health Care on a Shoestring: The Impact of Debt in Uganda by Trish Hegarty)

Photograph by Vicky Luyima.

Health Care on a Shoestring:
the Impact of Debt in Uganda

Trish Hegarty

Emerging from almost two decades of civil conflict and political violence, Uganda is a country with a potentially promising future. Growth rates since 1989 ranged between seven and four per cent per annum[1] and its adherence to debt repayment schedules has made it a success story of the world's largest development donor, the World Bank.

The National Resistance Movement (NRM) government has implemented a radical multi-layered system of democracy reaching down to village level, and its policy plans have a strong sense of social and economic direction.

But the outline potential cannot disguise the reality that Uganda is the world's fourth poorest country. Ninety per cent of national wealth is eaten up by debt, and its social and economic infrastructure has yet to recover from the disintegration of the seventies and eighties.

While World Bank representatives in Kampala paint a glowing picture of growing agricultural production and increased exports, their own figures estimate that more than half the population lives in poverty.[2]

Once near the top of the league table in terms of health status and health services in Africa, Uganda is now close to the bottom.[3]

Its population is still deeply and visibly suffering the consequences of both past conflict and current poverty and consequent decline in health status. In Kampala, crowded shanty town-type dwellings with little or no sanitation aid the spread of infectious diseases. Life in rural areas - where ninety per cent of the population lives - offers similar or worse conditions, and with even more restricted access to health services.

There is no evidence to the visitor's naked eye that Uganda suffers from the sharp divide between the rich and the poor characteristic of many developed and developing nations. Even those in the growing professional classes have a poor standard of living, and consumer goods are largely unavailable, even in the capital.

Restrictions imposed on the Ugandan government under structural adjustment programmes limit health spending, and therefore the ability to develop public health programmes which could radically improve the health of the nation.

Recent History

Historically Uganda was home to diverse groups of people, mainly the Bantu in the fertile south, and successive migrations of pastoral groups in the less fertile north. The arrival of rival Catholic and Protestant missionaries followed that of Muslim Arab traders and European explorers, and, from the mid-nineteenth century, all three faiths struggled for religious and temporal power, creating divisions still apparent in modern Uganda.

The government elected at independence in 1962, a loose coalition of southern and northern political parties, was led by Obote, who four years later abolished traditional kingdoms, banned political parties, introduced detention without trial, and promulgated a new constitution.

In 1971, Obote's regime was terminated in a coup led by the military leader Idi Amin Dada and his supporters within the army. Thousands of officers perceived as loyal to the Obote government were killed. The expulsion of Asians in 1972 helped to undermine the Amin regime's economic base in the long run, though it was initially popular with many Ugandans.

Amin was driven out in 1979, and two years of coups, selective killings, looting, famine, and outbreaks of disease followed. Although Obote was returned to power in 1980, it was perceived by many people in Uganda to have been a rigged election. The insecurity and murders continued, as did the disintegration of public services and administrative structures.

In 1986, the NRM came to power, and, while new conflicts emerged in the northern regions of the country, the majority of the districts embarked upon the difficult process of recovery. By 1992, a relative peace had been secured in Uganda, although the north remains neglected, poor, and subject to instability. Without a deliberate policy to promote economic development in the north, the potential for old political and social divisions to be exploited will remain a threat to the current fragile peace.

The Economic Context

Prior to 1971 Uganda had promising economic prospects. A wide range of subsistence crops were grown, and cotton and coffee provided export income. Manufacturing, though relatively small, was growing and contributed to the economic base.

With the expulsion of Asian business people in the early 1970s, the sector collapsed. Uganda's capital, Kampala, is today characterised by the dilapidated houses of these departed business people, now housing the growing - though far from affluent - indigenous professional classes. By 1980 commerce was in a state of crisis, and, in agriculture, only the subsistence farming sector had survived.

Measures to stabilise the economy, with IMF support, were undertaken in June of 1981, but by 1984 when negative growth rates of minus 8.5 per cent were recorded, IMF support had ended.

Since 1986, when the NRM government took power, economic

growth has been impressive - reaching seven per cent in 1989, and averaging at around four per cent in the 1990s. Agricultural production has increased and continues to expand against a background of declining export receipts.

In 1987, the NRM government committed itself to an IMF assisted economic recovery programme. A Structural Agreement Facility (SAF) was introduced, aimed at liberalising markets, adjusting exchange rates with inflation rates, increasing interest rates, and harmonising development expenditure.

But the diversification and monetisation of the agricultural sector championed by the World Bank and the IMF have serious implications for women, who traditionally, derive few benefits from cash crop agriculture. As a general rule, it is men who determine which crops will be grown. They also control the cash rewards.

And although rural women produce most of the country's food supply and provide seventy per cent of rural labour, their limited access to money means they face serious discrimination in benefitting from public services such as health and education when such services are available only on the payment of cash - in the name of cost-sharing.

Health Status of the Population

Uganda's public health system was once regarded as one of the finest in Africa. Clinics and mission hospitals which supplemented government facilities, provided a variety of services including nutrition, disease control, and family planning programmes.

As successive wars racked the country, health services broke down, doctors and professionals were killed, fled, or expelled, and health centres and hospitals were subjected to looting and destruction.

Not surprisingly, infant mortality increased, preventable disease claimed more under-fives, maternal mortality escalated, and life expectancy fell dramatically, reversing the steady progress which had been made since the 1960s. Today Uganda's social indicators are amongst the worst in the world.

Health Summary	1960,	1975,	1991	1992
Population per Physician:	N/A	9,210	25,000	N/A
Infant Mortality Rate:	133	109	118	111
Under 5 Mortality Rate:	223	173	190	185
Life Expectancy:	43	50	46	45
Maternal Mortality Rate:	N/A	N/A	5 per	5.5 per
(Per live birth)			1,000	1,000

Percentage of Children Immunised:	1991	1995
(less than 1 yr)		
Measles:	74%	77%
DDT (third dose):	77%	79%
Polio:	76%	79%
TB:	99%	100%

According to recent statistics, malaria constitutes twenty-five per cent of all new cases of treatment, with respiratory diseases comprising fifteen per cent of all treatment given. The incidence of HIV/AIDS is not known, though estimates suggest nearly eight per cent of Uganda's seventeen million people are HIV-positive, and HIV/AIDS related illnesses probably account for over thirty per cent of all hospital admissions.[4]

According to Sr Ursula, manager of Kitovu Hospital in the Masaka district, what these statistics do not show is that in some parts of Uganda, and to the south in particular, there are communities facing an incidence rate for HIV/AIDS of thirty per cent or more. The voluntary hospital reports increases in cerebral and cryptococcal meningitis, respiratory and urinary tract infections, all of which are associated with HIV/AIDS infection and immunosuppression.

Kitovu Hospital runs a mobile health clinic as the main hospital cannot cope with extra patients, which seeks to serve also those who cannot make it into the hospital. Accompanying one of the clinics to a remote rural community brought the reality of the disease in these areas sharply into focus for me. The medical staff monitor the progress of their patients, distribute medicines, and bring the comfort of regular personal contact through one-to-one counselling.

A group of close to forty villagers waited patiently for the arrival of the nurses, whom they greeted with warmth and excitement. They are largely patients with HIV/AIDS-related illnesses. The sight of the group this size might not be out of place in a Dublin AIDS clinic, but in an isolated country area it brings home the harsh truth that the disease is endemic in parts of Uganda.

Sr Ursula says that the communities in the Masaka district are facing massive social and health consequences from the high rate of HIV/AIDS infection. She explained that many of the communities are Catholic, and that the use of condoms to prevent the spread of the disease is not endorsed by the local priests and members of the church's hierarchy. She herself encourages their use as she is daily made painfully aware of the consequences of infection. But according to hospital workers, even where individuals in hospitals or in clinics encourage condom use as a preventative measure, women say that men, including husbands who may be unfaithful, will not use them.

As a consequence, the infection is spreading rapidly through the villages, and many women are left to bring up children alone on the death of their husbands from AIDS-related illnesses. I visited the homes of many women who had neither the strength nor the means to visit even the mobile clinic.

One woman, with newborn triplets, two-year-old twins, and two other children under eight, was herself infected with the virus, and her husband was seriously ill from AIDS. Their illness meant they were unable to grow their subsistence or cash crops, and dire poverty and malnutrition had resulted. The two-year-old twins looked like infants, while the woman, who did not wish to be named, was haggard with malnourishment.

In another village, an hour's drive away and accessible only through dirt tracks and paths through the scrub, a woman lived on her own with just a tiny dirt patch of land to grow crops. After her husband had died from an AIDS-related illness, his family threw her out of her house and left her to build a new hut wherever she could. Only the help of her neighbours keeps her from starvation.

Behind her hut, the picture is even more grim. An eleven-year-old boy is the head of a household of three children, orphaned by the death of both parents from the virus. The boy has given up school to raise the crops of coffee and groundnuts, and look after his younger sisters. He is not physically able to continue to harvest the coffee crop which was his parents' only source of cash.

A support programme from Kitovu hospital enables the girls to attend school, and provides the family with occasional cash for essentials like salt and soap. All three children suffer from regular bouts of malaria, and get little support from nearby villagers, who are already burdened with dependents. There is no apparent health and social services structure to support the children, whose closed faces bear obvious signs of emotional deprivation.

There is a growing number of single-headed and child-headed households where poverty is exacerbated by the decrease in earning potential, leaving children in particular more open to illnesses such as malaria.

The Department of Health's policy advisor admits that the government sponsored AIDS prevention programme is not impacting in such rural areas, and that health structures in remote regions are of the most basic.

Health Status of Women

The role that women play in traditional Ugandan society is commonly defined as one of subservience to men. According to FIDA (the International Federation of Women Lawyers), based in Kampala, many of the growing number of professional women in Kampala choose not to marry because of these traditional roles.

While the work FIDA does in seeking legal justice and equality for women is financially and politically supported by the government, this has little impact in the rural areas. In districts like Masaka, the subservience expected of women increases the difficulties they face in getting men to wear condoms, and so HIV/AIDS rates continue to climb.

Household surveys in Uganda indicate that women fare no worse than men in health terms, though this does not take account of illnesses relating specifically to reproductive health. Pregnancy, of course, is not an illness, but women may require medical attention during their pregnancy and need access to trained delivery personnel who can identify risks and refer patients during the pregnancy.

UNICEF figures indicate that about twenty-six per cent of women deliver in health institutions with the assistance of trained personnel, but what is on offer in these institutions varies widely between districts. On average, thirty-one per cent of those who do not deliver in health units are assisted by traditional birth attendants, while a higher number of women deliver in their own homes without any specialised assistance.[5]

Although more women deliver with the help of these traditional practitioners than in health units or hospitals, many of these attendants will have had little or no medical training. They will, however, have been trained in the use of traditional herbal medicine for both ante-natal and post-natal treatment.

Dr Tom Barton is an American doctor who practises and researches widely on health in Uganda. He points out that however positively one views the expertise of these traditional practitioners, maternal mortality rates are invariably higher in countries and areas where there is restricted access to referral centres and personnel trained in identifying risks.

With the high numbers of patients delivering with untrained personnel, who do not form any part of a government recording sytem, it is difficult to be accurate about the incidence of maternal mortality. Figures from Kampala hospitals indicate that maternal mortality is around 2.65 per 1,000 live births, but these figures relate only to the twenty-six per cent of mothers who deliver at health units or hospitals.

The major causes of death in pregnancy are haemorrhage, infections, pre-eclampsia and eclampsia, obstructed labour, and abortion - self-induced or spontaneous. These causes are generally related to poor hygiene and inadequate care rather than physical complications at birth. Malaria and anaemia also pose a serious threat to pregnant women. Basic community-based public health programmes could help reduce the threat from all these causes, yet such programmes are not run on a comprehensive nationwide basis, and model programmes - both in Kampala and outside the city - are run only with the financial assistance of agencies like Oxfam, and the Irish Bilateral Aid programme.

The Health System

The health system inherited at Independence in 1962 was based upon a network of state and voluntary hospitals and health centres, well distributed throughout the country.[6] These services and their expansion in the 1960s concentrated on curative care. Innovative primary health care programmes only began to be developed by the end of the decade, to be disrupted by successive conflicts.

The two decades of fighting left the health system in tatters, structurally and financially. 'The loss of key health personnel, destabilisation of civil institutions, and the interruption of the health debate within Uganda, and between Africa and the rest of the world, all contributed to the weakening of the health system.'[7]

Today, it is difficult to get a clear picture of the health service. There is little evidence that even a basic primary care system is in operation anywhere in the country, even if the physical infrastructure of the old system still technically exists. Local reports indicate that the physical infrastructure of the health service still exists, although seriously neglected in the recent past. According to 'Children and Women in Uganda: A Situational Analysis',[8] the large cadre of trained staff could provide a better health care service if given refresher training, equipment, supervision, and most importantly, adequate salaries.

The Ugandan government has 792 health facilities, which in theory provide free medical treatment to all. However, most health units and hospitals are in a state of poor repair; many patients must bring their own mattresses and linen on admission, and often relatives have to travel miles to bring food.

There are in addition 145 non-governmental hospitals and health units, most of which are attached to religious missions. These facilities usually charge at least a small fee. The services offered in health units, especially those run by the government, are often inadequate, but the majority of Ugandans still turn to them for curative services, even though they may first have sought treatment outside the formal system.

Services are more widely available and generally of a better standard in the capital Kampala, but over ninety per cent of the population live in rural areas or slums and are therefore unable to avail of these facilities.

According to Matthew Jowett, an economist with several years experience of health management and planning in East Africa, 'health systems in Africa, since the mid- to late 1980s, have been undergoing fundamental changes in the way they are organised and financed. International donor pressure, which has manifested itself primarily in terms of structural adjustment policies, has had several knock-on effects for the health sector.

'The distribution of skilled health professionals in rural parts of East Africa has for many years been a major concern. As a result of current reforms, wages in the health sector are so low that few of the more skilled health professionals will turn down an opportunity to leave for the private sector, which is being promoted under government policies of decentralisation. As the private sector survives only on profit, so the services they provide are concentrated where the wealthy live. In other words they tend to serve only urban populations rather than rural areas where where the majority of people, and the poor in particular, live'.

Only about twenty-seven per cent of the population lives within five kilometres of a health unit, while forty-three per cent live more than ten kilometres away from any facility. In the North, only twenty-three per cent of inhabitants have a health unit within five kilometres of their home and forty-three per cent within ten kilometres.[9]

Public transport in rural - and some urban - areas is limited or non-existent so most people will walk to a health unit for treatment. It will take a healthy adult two hours to walk ten kilometres; a sick person or mother carrying a child may take twice as long.

This factor alone influences the decisions of mothers to seek or not to seek health care, especially preventative services. The vast majority of low-income women barely have enough time in a day to complete their daily duties of caring for family, farm, and community, never mind an additional four hours travel time alone to visit a clinic. According to Jowett, 'in Uganda, mother and child services and family planning services are still free, which is crucial'.

Aside from the health problems of the Ugandan people, ongoing settlement of refugees from neighbouring countries, mainly Sudan, is imposing further demands on the health care system of the country.

The provision of health care - and other support - by aid agencies to Sudanese refugee camps in the north of the country, has occasionally caused resentment amongst the local people who face worse conditions in their own villages. The current strategy in the north at least is for integrated settlement programmes, with the provision of health and other facilities accessible to all including the local population.

The Three-Year Plan

The Ugandan government has a three-year health plan which aims to improve existing health service provision, and to provide a broader public health programme. Ongoing projects in the improvement of sanitation and hygiene will undoubtedly do much to reduce the incidence of, for example, diarrhoeal diseases. Many of these programmes are, however, dependent upon outside funding, while the bulk of government expenditure on health services goes to health units and hospitals, in the absence of a comprehensive primary health programme.

With the health service still grossly underdeveloped and underfunded - preventing the largely rural population from having a locally accessible health service - the imposition of user charges can deny access to those who could otherwise use local services. The issue of user fees is not a straightforward one.

In principle, the Ugandan government is opposed to a health service which is accessible only to those who have money to pay for it; in practice, user fees have been informally introduced by clinics because it is the only way to guarantee an income for staff.

In parts of Uganda, health units have not been functioning or are unable to provide a proper service because the staff have not been paid, and either they do not turn up for work or are privately selling essential medical supplies and drugs to provide an income. Unofficial charges have frequently been imposed for services which should technically be free by staff who have not received a salary payment for months.

The explanation offered by a senior Department of Finance official was that salary payments were delayed because of problems inherent in the system of administration, which is both antiquated and still in a state of recovery from decades of conflict.

This problem is acknowledged, and in a sense forced the government to consider the introduction of fees for health services, a course of action favoured by the World Bank and the IMF.

Matthew Jowett contends that 'the most worrying thing about the introduction of fees is the effect they have on those who are most in need of health care. Clearly the poor lose out the most, despite the commitment of governments to exempt the poor from payment. There is, as yet, no effective exemption system in rural East Africa protecting the poor. Evidence from Ghana shows that following the introduction of user fees, the rural population as a whole, and the elderly in general, used far less health care than before. In Ghana, women used more health care than men after fees, whilst the opposite was true in Kenya. The effect of fees can be complicated, and an understanding of how much control women have of cash is crucial'.

The NRM government is not characterised by a slavish commitment to fiscal rectitude at all costs, or to serving the interests of a wealthy elite. What comes across from senior department officials and advisors is a government faced with social and economic reconstruction needs which they are incapable of meeting, due to the enormous burden of inherited and accumulated debt, and crippling repayment schedules.

Conclusion

Under its current regime of foreign debt repayments, the Ugandan government is obliged to control public spending. These limitations inevitably restrict the amount of money available to support the health sector. Even more serious, in terms of equity and the welfare of the poor, is the demand of the international financial institutions that foreign debt must be given priority.

In 1992, Uganda spent more than five times more on debt repayment than on the health of its people. In 1994, Uganda was scheduled to pay $162 million in debt service payments. This represents over four-fifths of the country's export earnings. This compares to the $120 million the government spent on health and education in that same year. [10]

Nearly two-thirds of Uganda's 2.26 billion debt is owed to multilateral institutions like the World Bank and the IMF which, in spite of the drastic situation, refuse to take any initiatives in writing off these debts.

The government is aware of the need to inject funds into rural health units, public health, and health education - particularly on HIV/AIDS - and that the poorest are suffering most from their failure to provide such funding. But the government is also tied into a level of foreign debt repayments that prohibits them from allocating such necessary funds.

The consequences of failing to meet scheduled debt repayments could be an economic and political isolation which Uganda cannot risk.

The inability to adequately fund the health services is impacting on the health and welfare of the nation as a whole, and women and children in particular.

In interviews with IMF representatives based in Uganda, it was accepted that any country's ability to develop its economy, particularly an economy based largely on agriculture, will be restricted by the state of the nation's health.

More surprisingly, they also accepted that the 'rising tide lifts all boats' concept currently offers no hope to those so poor and isolated that they can neither grow cash crops nor gain access to health services.

Unfortunately, this awareness has not yet been translated into a policy of debt cancellation for this devastated country, despite the fact that the failure to do so poses a serious obstacle to lasting development in Uganda.

SOURCE: *UNICEF (1993), 'The State of the World's Children', New York: Oxford University Press World Bank (1993), 'World Development Report: Investing in Health' New York: Oxford University Press. UNDP, 'Human Development Report: 1995', New York: Open University Press, 1995.*

NOTES:
1. World Bank Report, 'Uganda, Growing out of Poverty', 1993.
2. *ibid.*
3. LSTM, 1994.
4. Gaigals, 1994.
5. UNICEF, 1991.
6. LSTM,1994.
7. LSTM, 1994:vii.
8. UNICEF, 1991.
9. UNICEF,1991.
10. Watkins, 1994.

Focus on

Ugandan Women Organising

Penny Cabot

An interview with Maude Mugisha, chairperson of The Uganda Women's Network, with Penny Cabot, chairperson of Banúlacht, Irish Women For Development.

Penny: Maude, can you tell me a bit about your work in Uganda?

Maude: I work with a woman's organisation called 'Action for Development', a member of Ugandan Women's Network (UWONET) - a network of local development organisations. UWONET focuses on Ugandan economic policies, economic reforms, and the impact of economic reform on women in particular. I'm in Ireland to share experiences of what we as women see as the effects of stabilisation and adjustment programmes.

Penny: What has UWONET discovered about the impact of adjustment on Ugandan women's lives?

Maude: We have done some research on the effects of adjustment on women in Arua District in northern Uganda in relation to agriculture, education and health care.

Structural adjustment has brought in the liberalisation of the market for many cash crops: for instance, the liberalisation of the marketing of cotton from the Lint Marketing Board has handed the marketing function to private monopoly buyers who pay less than the cost of production. This restricts women's economic effectiveness.

Secondly we found that tobacco processing, marketing, extension services and credit were all organised by a vertically integrated private monopoly that often paid farmers late and 'in kind'. The tobacco is often inconsistently graded to the disadvantage of the farmer.

Even these limited producer price incentives by-pass women because women do not control the revenue from cash crops. In addition, women have little control of the critical resources, such as land or tractors, which are needed to produce cash crops. These resources are controlled by men. Women's access to credit is limited because they do not own

61

land or have control of cash to use as collateral to secure loans. Women lag at the rear of the production and technology frontier because they are either ignored and not admitted to extension classes, or because they have no time to attend such classes to learn the technology and propose modifications to meet their needs.

The allocation of often scattered small pieces of land to women to grow food, wastes labour and time as women have to move between pieces of land. Also women need the husband's consent to sell part of the food they grow. Even in those cases where women take food to the market and sell it themselves, they still need their husband's consent to use the money.

In the area of health care, local communities have been dragged into a cost sharing arrangement in order to have access to health care - building hospitals, paying salary incentives to health personnel and buying equipment.

The user fee scheme, as a structural adjustment policy, was meant to increase the availability of services. However, our data collection did not show any expansion of services or improvement in quality of the services due to the policy.

Respondents reported, that when the public was asked to pay, those who were able opted for higher quality services in missionary hospitals. Those unable to pay used traditional birth attendants, traditional healers and self medication. The services of the public health care units are therefore likely to get abandoned and to deteriorate further.

As far as financial cut-backs in education are concerned, school drop out begins as early as Primary Four due to school fee constraints. Parents must contribute to textbooks, exercise books, the building fund and staff welfare dues. Furthermore, demands come through fund-raising funtions to pay for the construction and maintenance of the physical infrastructure. The above charges, along with school fees and uniforms make education very expensive.

Girls attempting to cope with increased income-generating activities start school when they are older than boys and attend irregularly, leading to poor performance. Some have to raise resources for school on their own. Many drop out early to get married.

Penny: What do you think the Fourth World Conference on Women in Beijing might achieve?

Maude: As African women we have three main concerns: firstly, the need for women's economic empowerment - if women had more money then the situation would be much better than it is today. Most of the oppression that the African woman suffers is because she is poor, so we focus on poverty and economic empowerment for women. The Ugandan Women's Network is presenting a workshop on economic empowerment for women in Beijing, specifically focusing on African women.

Secondly, we are focusing on girl children. We feel that the hope of Africa lies in the support and welfare of the girl child. Our concern is that the girl child does not enjoy the same opportunities as her brothers.

Thirdly we are focusing on the rights of women, especially the rights of property ownership. Most important is that women's rights will be recognised as human rights for women throughout Africa.

Maude Mugisha of the Ugandan Women's Network meeting President Mary Robinson, during Maude's visit to Ireland at the invitation of the Debt and Development Coalition of Ireland.

Photograph by Tommy Clancy.

Penny: Are you optimistic that Beijing will make changes for women?

Maude: Yes, I think it is possible, but these changes will not necessarily be brought out in Beijing but in the follow-up process afterwards. We feel that Beijing offers a unique opportunity for women to discuss these issues, and develop solidarity among women and support for each other. It is important for women to use Beijing to develop strategies so that the issues raised will be followed up and implemented, by the participating governments in 1996 and thereafter.

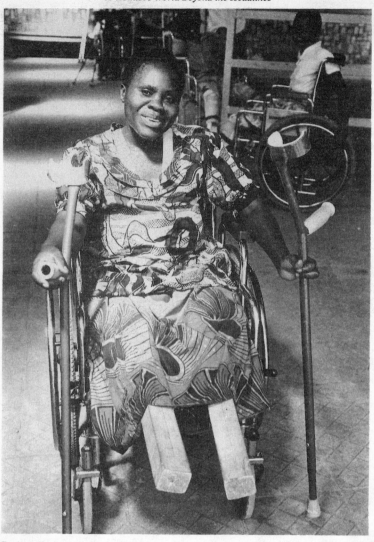

Caritas Kayigawa, thirty-four years old, is a patient at Kigali's central hospital. 'I stepped on a mine on 7 October 1994. It was near where I used to live in Jari, part of Kigali. I was taken to a hospital and then at the end of January, after my wounds had healed, I was brought here. Before the war I had four children, a husband and a home. My brothers were killed, my home was destroyed and when we were running away and hiding I lost my husband and three of my children. I was left alone with just one child, a three-year-old. I don't know what happened to my husband and my other children - if they were killed or if they left the country. Now a neighbour is looking after the little one, as I can't. I am very lucky to have a good neighbour.' (Women and Conflict: The Challenges, the Future for Women in Rwanda by Breeda Hickey)

Photograph by Jenny Matthews.

Women and Conflict: the Challenges, the Future for Women in Rwanda

Breeda Hickey

'The majority of women have suffered profoundly; we have suffered in our bodies - through blows, starvation, rape, infection, pregnancy - and in our hearts; many of our loved ones have disappeared without trace, and our deceased have not been afforded decent burials. Now, we are trying to survive physically and psychologically, despite the few members of family left to us. Each day is a struggle against hunger or madness. The two torment us. To survive we have formed small self-help organisations, which allow us to look for solutions to material problems, while at the same time giving each other moral support to carry on.'[1]

Violence against Women: a Global Issue
Following the assassination of the President of Rwanda in April 1994, Hutu extremists embarked on a campaign of genocide in that country. Over one million people lost their lives, and millions more became refugees in Tanzania, Burundi and Zaire. In the aftermath of such devastation, it is crucial that we consider the specific and particular implications of conflict and violence for women.

Here in Ireland, we are finally enjoying a fragile peace, and it is certain many Irish women will find echoes of their own experiences in the experiences of Rwandese women, and women all over the world who have endured violence, be it domestic, civil, national or international.

Violence, which can be defined as an assault on a person's physical and mental integrity, is an underlying feature of all societies, an undercurrent running through social interaction at many levels. In situations of war or violent conflict, all civilians suffer. However, women experience conflict and violence in several ways, related explicitly to the gender division of rights, roles and responsibilities. Class, religious and ethnic differences overlay this gender-related experience.

In all countries, including those sympathetic to women's equality, women remain second-class citizens. Women suffer infringement of their basic rights as human beings, and live with the ever-present threat or experience of physical and sexual violence. While perpetrators of violence are perceived to be predominantly male, there are increasing instances of violence by women against other women, illustrated below in the Rwanda experience.

Violence may often come from those from whom one most expects protection: community elders, state institutions. This is again illustrated graphically in the Rwandan crisis. Violence against women is used to keep women in their place, to limit their opportunities to live, learn, work and care as full human beings, to hamper their capabilities to organise and claim their rights.

Violence is a major obstacle to women's empowerment, and to their full participation in shaping the economic, social and political life in their countries. Violence takes both a physical and a mental toll; it erodes self-esteem and self-confidence, limiting women's capacity to solve their own problems, as well as their capacity to develop relationships with others.

Worldwide, a high proportion of incidences of violence against women take place in the home, making the home one of the most dangerous places for women: in the USA battery from husbands and partners is the leading cause of injury to adult women; in Africa, more than ninety million women and girls are victims of genital mutilation.

Domestic abuse of women and girl children also includes the denial of health care and education to girl children and women, early and forced marriage, exclusion of female household members from participation in decision making, and exclusion of widows from the extended family.

State violence condemns women to inferior roles in society, from a perception of girl children as somehow inferior, to the differences in educational opportunities afforded them in comparison to their brothers; to the limited life opportunities presented to many women throughout the world to actualise their true and full potential. In this, the church is often complicit with the state, seeking to control women through controlling their bodies, particularly with respect to reproductive rights, and in enforcing social control, for example marriage should be for life; divorce is not allowed, or if allowed it is at the husband's discretion.

Research on aid planning in emergency situations has shown that a community's ability to survive disasters depends on the extent to which it has minimised 'vulnerabilities' and maximised 'capacities'. Strengthening women's status and capacities contributes to the community's ability to withstand the effects of disasters. Programmes of assistance delivered by aid agencies may be conceived with the best of intentions, but often fail to disaggregate their target populations, or take into account the 'felt' needs of the community.

In a world where the number of emergencies is becoming larger, more frequent and more complex, there is an understandable pressure to 'be seen to be doing something'. However, aid delivery systems often establish power structures and dependencies which last long after a crisis is over, and if these systems - as is often the case - reduce women's power in relation to men, development can be set back years. In simple numerical terms, women and their dependants form the majority of the vast numbers of people affected by wars today, so interventions which do not help them meet their basic needs and responsibilities can result in great and needless suffering.

Recognition of women's needs and a gender-based analysis of an emergency situation are essential starting points if an aid intervention is to be effective in the short term and have positive impacts in long-term development. Because women play the crucial role in sustaining their families and communities in times of crisis, aid which helps them to function effectively is particularly useful; it is efficient aid. There is also a preventive aspect to aid which is gender-sensitive: women are more vulnerable than men to disasters largely because of their subordinate social position, so improving this reduces their future vulnerability.

In the Aftermath of Genocide in Rwanda

The subordinate social position of women, particularly in developing countries, means that women typically have few property or land rights. In Rwanda, many women are now in a very precarious economic situation. Many have had their homes razed to the ground and struggle to put a roof over their heads and the heads of their children (if they have survived). Their property was looted during the destruction, and many who had to flee their small plot of land have since returned to find it occupied by others.

The costs of accessing legal representation and the fact that the law is not clear about property rights of women means that many of these women will continue to live in an uncertain situation most likely for the rest of their lives. Added to this is the complicated issue of who exactly is entitled to claim land in Rwanda today - there have been such movements of population over the last three decades that often two or three different families can lay claim to the one plot of land. For an illiterate peasant woman to have a voice in this situation will be extremely difficult.

In Rwanda, there has been a significant increase in the numbers of households primarily or exclusively dependent on women's labour to survive. This places another burden on women's shoulders at a time when they are experiencing emotional and economic stress. When men are absent, the full weight of family survival falls on women who are compelled, and, ironically, also enabled, to take on roles from which they may have been excluded in more peaceful times. Although the personal costs to women can be high in terms of physical and emotional stress, the gains in confidence, self-worth and powerfulness can be enormous.

The demographic changes which have taken place in Rwanda have led the government to acknowledge the potential contribution that women can make to society and to call on employers and those in positions of authority, particularly in the field of education, to integrate women more fully into society. The government acknowledges that a lot remains to be done, because of the often inferior education afforded women and the handicaps that they struggle with in trying to find employment.

Added to the economic hardship is the psychological trauma. According to Prudentienne Nambajimana, from Kigali, 'As a result of what has happened in my country, we are all suffering. She who has managed to escape death, now suffers for lack of food, a home, a family, and also has health problems because of the memories of what has gone on in her life ...'[2]

Many women have lost all members of their families and have been forced to witness their deaths. In Rwanda, there had been a lot of intermarriage between Hutus and Tutsis. If a Hutu woman married a Tutsi man, their children were considered Tutsi. During the genocide, many Hutu women in this situation were forced from their homes, forced to witness the violent deaths of their husbands and children, to watch their homes being destroyed and their belongings looted. For other women, there is the mental torture of not knowing what happened to other family members; many families were split up when people had to flee and now many live in hope that maybe, just maybe, their children are alive and living in one of the refugee camps outside the country or even in a centre for unaccompanied children within Rwanda. There are agencies working to reunify families, and the waiting and the hoping goes on.

Sexual Violence as a Crime of War

'Another thing that shocked me was the way they (the militia) killed women: firstly they raped them and afterwards, to kill them, they knifed them, starting with their private parts ...' *Prudentienne Nambajimana*

A conspiracy of silence has kept rape and forced sexual relations off the agenda until very recently. Now this is changing: safety from rape is recognised as a right, and protecting women from rape and addressing its consequences are challenges that are being faced in Bosnia and Rwanda to mention but a few. In Rwanda, rape was used as an instrument of violence and humiliation, and an attempt at ethnic conquest. One example cited in African Rights is of a woman abducted by an interahamwe (militiaman) who kept her for two days, and then took her to the road block when he went to do night patrols. She was repeatedly raped by different interahamwe; when she became very weak, she was given to a Twa (pygmy) to keep - intended as a humiliation in the social context of Rwanda.

This practice of 'handing on' women to men from groups that are looked down upon was confirmed in several eye witness accounts.

Men who abducted women often disagreed with one another over the fate of their captives. A doctor told the story of a young boy he had treated. The young boy had been hiding with his younger sister in a bush. Some men walked by and heard the sound of movement from the bushes. One of them shouted: 'You woman, come out. We can see you!' The girl panicked and came out of her hiding place. One of the men raped her. A second man wanted to rape her, but the first man objected and an argument broke out. A third shot her, saying it was the easiest way to settle the dispute.

Many women were raped before being killed with machetes; others were raped by marauding Hutu militiamen and allowed to live, in the hope that they would bear Hutu children. Many have given birth, but the pregnancy was a time of hardship and shame, and a reminder that the father was often the same person who callously butchered their families before their eyes; and the baby is helpless and innocent but often unwanted and rejected. Some of these newborn babies have been abandoned; some have almost certainly been killed; and others placed immediately in already overstretched orphanages.

The impact of violence on women's mental health is hard to over-estimate. Violence erodes their self-esteem and self-confidence, and their ability to form new relationships. Esther Mujawayo is painfully clear: 'most of us who survived are physically handicapped as a result of machete blows, many were raped and now must endure the consequences such as AIDS, pregnancy, and unwanted babies. For these women it is like a never-ending nightmare: you suffer in your mind ... your heart ... your body ... And the worst is that you are ashamed of it. You were a victim and now society makes you feel guilty.'

Throughout the world, in war-time as in peace-time, women are reluctant to talk openly about rape. Religious, cultural and social norms discourage women from expressing their feelings, no matter how painful the physical, mental and emotional distress they are suffering. Rwanda is no different and the need for support and counselling is particularly acute. The need to reintegrate raped women into the social fabric is great, but must be done in such a way that these women do not have a reduced social status on account of their experiences. In some parts of Uganda, for example, women who had been raped had no alternative subsequently but to turn to prostitution.

Violence against women is a serious aggravating factor in the spread of AIDS. Women who have been raped run high risks of HIV infection, and this must certainly be the case in Rwanda.

The nature of the conflict in Rwanda was such that it affected all levels of society and turned neighbour against neighbour; woman against woman. People and institutions traditionally considered to be refuges turned out to be false havens. Thousands of people fled to churches and schools in the hope that these buildings would be respected. However, more Rwandese citizens died in churches and parish buildings than anywhere else. The violation of churches as places of sanctuary was something wholly new and totally shocking in Rwanda. Although it is a very small minority, there is even evidence of priests wielding machetes and guns against their own parishoners; of nuns who refused to treat the injured; other instances of priests and local government authorities betraying people's whereabouts to the marauding gangs. There are well documented instances of school teachers leading the attacks against pupils and their families.

There is evidence that women, both well educated and illiterate, participated in the genocide. This undermines our assumptions that women don't murder. Women were involved at all levels - planning, organising, identifying targets, even killing with their own hands. Girls in their teens followed the bands of militia, robbing the dead of their clothes, while older women ululated and danced, cheerleaders for the killers. Hutu extremists wrote a set of 'ten commandments' outlining their ideology, where the ills of the country were laid largely at the feet of Tutsi women.

'As a woman, what made me most sad was to see other women with machetes in their hands, manning the roadblocks with men, ready to kill other women and their children without a thought, and happy then to strip those women naked.'[3]

Rwanda's current Minister for the Family and Women, Aloisie Inyumba, says she was shocked when she learned that women had participated in the genocide. 'I couldn't believe it because traditionally our culture respected women so much, and they have a moral value for children. It showed me how low the moral degeneration of our country has gone.'[4]

One of the most tragic aspects of any conflict situation is the effect it has on children. In Rwanda, a whole generation of children has been scarred by the events of 1994. A substantial portion of children who survived attacks have suffered horrific wounds - hands or arms struck off by machetes, Achilles' tendons severed, throats slashed, heads and faces cut, teeth smashed in and bones broken. Children have watched their parents and siblings being macheted and knifed to death in front of their eyes. On the other hand, some young boys have also been accomplices in murder. They have directly participated in massacres, macheting other children and even attacking adults.

The terror has left more than physical wounds - many children lost the power of speech; some who were forbidden from talking while in hiding have had to relearn their vocabulary; some stare into space with vacant, haunted, unseeing eyes; some of them have refused to eat and died. The crowded centres for unaccompanied children, both inside and outside Rwanda, cannot hope to provide adequate psychological support and love to help these children. Agencies working to reunite families face a huge task, which is really only the beginning.

Rwandan society will have to arrive at a mechanism for helping children to overcome the trauma they have endured and reintegrate into society. The work is underway: school-going children are encouraged by their teachers to talk about the experiences they have lived, and to use art therapy as a means to expression.

The Demand for Justice
'I cannot finish without citing another terrible consequence - in the past, all Rwandans lived as brothers and sisters; now we hunt one another away - there is a want of friendship and trust between people. Maliciousness and hate exist now.'[5]

Two years after the outbreak of genocide, Rwanda is a dislocated society - psychologically, socially, economically. Effort has been made by the government through reburial ceremonies to help people grieve for their dead; certain churches will be designated as monuments to the tragedy of the genocide, lest anyone forget the true enormity of the crime. But people want and need more if they are to have any real chance of reconciliation and resuming a normal community life.

The International Tribunal has just issued eight indictments against people suspected of war crimes. Justice must be seen to be done this time. Many Rwandese are clutching at the hope that their country, and a sense of moral order, can be rescued by an act of justice. The imperative is to dispense justice, to tell the truth, and to end the culture of impunity for criminals.'We will never know peace if we keep covering up such unspeakable crimes. If the people responsible for what has happened are not punished, they will do it again and it will encourage others to take the same actions in the future. It is too painful even to contemplate the possibility that the people responsible for these crimes might escape justice.'[6] Lack of action in bringing the killers to justice is, in the words of one peasant, 'a seed for a future harvest of killing and war'.

Until justice is seen to be done, Rwandese women and men are in danger of continuing 'to live in a state of stuck', to borrow a phrase from the world of the physically disabled. Only then can Rwandese women and men take up the challenge of the other enormous tasks facing them, namely the reintegration of returnees, land and property rights, and allow the creation of space for new leaders to emerge; leaders who are capable of maintaining humanity and dignity, and who will help to forge a new identity for Rwanda.

NOTES:

1. Esther Majawayo, personal communication.
2. Prudentienne Nambajimana, personal communication.
3. *ibid.*
4. Aloisie Inyumba, Minister for the Family and Women in Rwanda, 'Death, Despair and Defiance'.
5. Prudentienne Nambajimana, personal communication.
6. Marc Rugenara, former and current Minister of Finance in Rwanda, 'Death, Despair and Defiance'.

BIBLIOGRAPHY:

Warnock, K 'Women, War and Humanitarian Intervention'. From ODI Newsletter, September 1995.
Hilsum, L 'Women Killers in Rwanda'. ODI Newsletter, Sept.1995.
O'Connell, H 'Women and Conflict', Oxfam Focus on Gender, Volume 1, Number 2 June 1993.
El-Bushra, J and Piza Lopez, E. 'Gender-related Violence: its scope and relevance'.
'Rwanda: Death, Despair and Defiance by African Rights', 1994, London: African Rights.

In urban Mozambique, employment for women is still largely limited to the informal sector. Employment within this sector, like fish selling, is low-paid, unskilled and insecure. (Brick by Brick: Rebuilding Mozambique by Maggie O'Kane)

Photograph by Jenny Matthews.

Brick by Brick:
Rebuilding Mozambique

Maggie O'Kane

Miss Angelina will be the first to get a house. We are forty miles outside Maputo, the capital of Mozambique, and the women, who are building the houses, making the bricks and mixing the cement, have decided that Angelina, the poorest, is in the most need of shelter.

It's all incredibly sane and civilised. We are surrounded by homes destroyed by men over a sixteen year period in a brutal war and now, the women with infinite patience, justice, and good humour have decided that Angelina is the one who should be helped first. Not for the first time, you wish to yourself in the charred, windswept, shanty town: 'if only ...'

The women in their tangerine plimsolls and bare feet have set up a cooperative building programme along the Matola Rivier at the village of Gaza. Their plan is to rebuild the homes that were destroyed during the war. They are all returned refugees from Swaziland and South Africa, who fled from sixteen years of civil war. Now they are back, literally rebuilding their country, with the assistance of one hundred and forty-five international relief agencies and millions of pounds of United Nations funds.

The cost of each house is around £500, according to the chief builder, Luis Nhantum. It takes eight hundred bricks and ten sheets of iron to construct it. Luis is one of the few men in sight on this desolate, arid piece of land. He directs the work amid dozens of women mixing cement and piling bricks, all ready to be laid for Miss Angelina's £500 house. He is very aware of the problems of ownership after the women have laboured to build the houses: 'Despite the women having done everything, their husbands wanted the houses to be in their names. For example the men would decide that the house should be in the name of Fabiao, although it was Maria who built it.'

The scene, despite the fact that civil war ended three years ago, looks not unlike the Bosnian landscape. Charred houses that have lain unoccupied for years and beside them the temporary huts that the returning refugees have erected. A Dutch aid agency has provided the money for basic building materials, and today the women are building for Angelina.

They have also rebuilt the school, and pay for the teachers by each family donating twenty pence a month for salaries.

Carlos Malthusa, the head teacher, gets paid some months, but not others. 'We are just beginning the rebuilding,' he says; 'it will take time.'

On the concrete floor of the school, the children lay out their few books on the back of the cotton cloths they spread on the floor. They are far away from any thoughts of desks, but the head teacher is cheerful; they have, after all, come a long way since 1992 when the civil war ended. Up to one million people died from fighting and war-related hunger and disease, in what could be described as one of the most brutal holocausts against ordinary human beings since World War Two.

Nearly two million fled the country and some four million were internally displaced. After ten years of fighting, a radical Marxist revolutionary movement succeeded in winning Mozambique's war of independence against its Portuguese colonisers in 1975. When the Portuguese handed over control of Mozambique in 1975 they stripped the country. Heavy machinery was taken with them, printers and typewriters were dumped in Maputo harbour, concrete was poured down lift wells and toilets; even the light bulbs were taken from government buildings. The Portuguese left behind a population that was ninety-five per cent illiterate.

It was from this starting point that the women's movement in Mozambique would develop.

But Rhodesia, then in the grip of Ian Smith's white government, sought to depose Frelimo (the Front for the Liberation of Mozambique) who had won power when the Portugese had granted independence. Smith was exercising revenge against the Frelimo for their rear-base support of the Zimbabwean freedom fighters. Fearful that the revolutionaries would destabilise the region, Ian Smith's government was responsible for the formation of the Movement of National Resistance (Renamo), which over the next sixteen years would contribute to the death of over 100,000 civilians. When Ian Smith lost power in Rhodesia, the South African government stepped in to continue to supply arms and mercenaries to Renamo.

The world largely turned a blind eye to what was happening in Mozambique until a USA state department report in 1988 firmly pointed the finger at Renamo. The horrors of the civil war went unreported for years. In an attempt to undermine the new government with its ambitious ideas of schools, medical centres and literacy campaigns, Renamo targeted hundreds of the new community centres around Mozambique, blowing the fragile new infrastructure back generations and blowing the emerging women's movement back into oblivion. It also mutilated a whole generation of Mozambique's newly liberated people. Rape, as in Bosnia, was used as a weapon of war. Mutilation of the vanquished by the victors was common in a war dreamt up by the old Rhodesian intelligence service and which prospered under the steady hand of the South African military.

The Renamo army comprised a large percentage of men and boys kidnapped from villages, and, according to a 1991 UNICEF report, 'The Cost of Survival', children as young as eight were used as porters. The report describes how the children were completely dependent on orders from the military, and complete obedience was demanded. Learning to kill became part of the child soldiers' training. Estevan, twelve, is quoted as follows: 'three bandits were making mistakes and falling behind. The bandits [Renamo] asked us what we should do with them. Jorge said they should be sent back to the base to work with the women. The bandits said they should be killed. They gave Jorge a bayonet. When Jorge did not move, one of the bandits cut his stomach with the bayonet. He gave him the bayonet back and this time he killed the three boys.'[1]

The Organisation for Mozambican Women (OMM) was born with the country's revolution, its main aim being to empower women by education. One of the leading members was Graca Machel. She was also wife to the country's revolutionary President, Samora Machel, and has won several international prizes and awards for her work with children. Of the founding of the Mozambican women's movement, she said in 1985: 'Women fought in the armed struggle, and this had a big influence on changing attitudes. It gave us confidence and made us realise what our role should be.'

The liberation of Mozambique's women was speeded up by women's farm cooperatives which were set up around the country by the Frelimo government. The new government also handed over some of the running of the country's judicial system to women justices of the peace. The first target of the fledgling women's movement in Mozambique was the 'lobolo', the bride price that was traditionally handed over by the husband to the bride's father. The prevailing attitude of: 'I've bought her so she's mine to do what I like with' led to widespread abuse, but over the past fifteen years, the 'lobolo' has been largely done away with.

A second major target of the fledgling women's movement in Mozambique was the widespread acceptance of polygamy. The Frelimo party backed their activists in the women's movement by passing party rules that forbade polygamous men from becoming party members or running for office. To those who had two or more wives before independence, the party turned a blind eye.

To some extent the OMM was simply an extension of the party; the action on 'lobolo' and on polygamy were both attacks on the traditional lifestyles of people, consistent with Frelimo's early policies of 'out with the old, in with the new' which had led to the targeting and undermining of many aspects of traditional life and authority.With regard to the issue of polygamy, it is still very widely practised in many parts of Mozambique, and many people regard it as part of their cultural and religious heritage.

What is needed is for legislation to take account of and enshrine the rights of second and subsequent wives.

Independence subsequently gave way to war, and now, in the first real year of peace after the October 1994 elections, it is plain to see how far back the civil war has pushed Mozambique's women. But now they are literally rebuilding their country brick by brick.

Through the trees near the village of Gaza, where the women are working to rebuild their homes, their lives, and their families, is the house of Eugina Vilunculos. Her house has no roof, and she is waiting patiently for the women she works with to decide when to build with her. For eight years, when the Renamo rebels were close to her village, she walked twenty miles a day, leaving every evening at dusk to go to safe areas away from attacks that came in the night. 'Once I left it late and I saw in the distance that they were coming. I was up in the tree picking oranges and then I was down in the street so fast that my breasts were flying everywhere, but I just kept running and running like crazy.

'Now that the war is over and we have come back to our village, life is a bit better to me, but the life is still difficult. Why? Because there are things in the shops but I don't have money to buy food to eat. Medicines are there in the hospital but I don't have money for treatment for the kids and myself.'

Despite years of walking, and 'running like crazy', Eugina has no desire to see scores settled. She does not even question the reason for the war. 'Politics!' she says. 'Politics! No, there is no vengeance in me. I don't know what it was about. Politics!'

Philip Clarke, an ebullient Argentinian who cuts through the UN-speak to shoot from the hip, is the director of the World Food Programme in Mozambique. He has worked in most of the world's trouble spots in the last ten years. He can compare Mozambique to Angola, to El Salvador, and in Mozambique he sees the women playing an essential role in reconstruction. Essential because they appear to be doing most of the work. Backed by some one hundred and forty-five international aid agencies, Mozambique relies on women to rebuild.

Mozambique has been one of the UN's success stories. Their main success was that they held the middle ground long enough to allow peace to be negotiated. The seven thousand UN troops in the country facilitated the elections and allowed for a negotiated peace. It would most likely have happened anyway with the Cold War over, South Africa's apartheid regime overturned, and President Banda gone from Malawi; neither side has the resources necessary to continue - less still win - the conflict. Since the war ended in 1992, death or revenge killings have been few and far between. The peace process has been remarkably calm and orderly, far exceeding expectations.

Yvonne wears a pink silk scarf. She is thirty-two and, unusually, has no children. Her story is, however, usual enough. During the war her uncle was chopped up by a machete and two of her brothers were killed in the fighting. Like most women she is also ready to forgive anything to return to a normal life.

Ask her why it happened, why the guerillas came and she gives the answer typical of the working women: 'they came to fight,' she says, shrugging her shoulders, 'the way men do.' I think to myself: she has no questions, no bitterness, no anger about the war. Neither does her husband.

Ask her about her life now and Yvonne has more to say. 'I lost a lot, I lost my house, I lost almost all my dishes, now I'm down to zero. Even if you come into my house I cannot give you a chair to sit on, because I don't have one.'

Outside the wind-swept hut, scrawny trees grow in rich red soil. She lives in a landscape punctuated with the charred houses that remain after the war. Houses that were destroyed and which are slowly being rebuilt as Yvonne and her husband try to make the best of things.

From her husband who spent eight years as a soldier, there is also no bitterness; no talk of revenge. He has lost six close friends and relatives in the war but he is ready to forgive. After the war both sides were kept in camps run by the United Nations while their weapons were taken. How, after years of war do the opposing soldiers feel about each other? 'I don't bear any grudge. It was a political conflict, it was nothing to do with us ordinary soldiers.' No anger? 'That's politics, that's the way things are. I don't have reasons to be angry - okay, I lost a lot of things, but that is politics.'

He speaks highly of the UN: 'during this period we learned how to be normal. The UN taught us how to be together. They paid our salaries, they set us up a trust fund to pay the soldiers. We could never have done it by ourselves. The government pension schemes they set up really helped us.'

To survive, they sell charcoal; the land has been dry, with insufficient rain for crops. Now Maunge Francisco dreams of a good job, to have some small animals - goats and chickens, that's all. A goat is $35 (£22), and if you really ask him to dream, his greatest dream he would like five goats.

After twenty years' development experience, Philip Clarke starts at the bottom to rebuild, and it is the women to whom he turns: 'I am convinced after all these years that things will have to come from the ground. If you impose it from the top it takes three times longer and costs three times as much than if you bring it in from below.'

Two shanty towns in Maputo are running a project to repair the roads. On the project Clarke prefers to use women workers. Ninety per cent of his workforce are women workers. 'We pay them in food and maybe about a dollar a day. The women are doing it first of all because they want to improve their own homes and places. To have a road where you can pass during the rainy season and to be able to feed the children. We carried out surveys in both shanty towns to ascertain what the people wanted: to be paid with money or to be paid with food. First they don't want to be paid just money, they want food and then matches and then vegetables.'

Clarke found that while such projects worked in the slums and towns, projects in the country didn't work. 'They don't have the time in the country. In Mozambique women don't just look after the family, they look after the land. They have to find the water, they have to weed, to plant, they have to do the whole thing about the family. It is not possible for them to carry out extra work.

'Women, because of their families, will work for food. In these projects when we secured funds and increased the wages we got the men wanting jobs - but when the work was paid in food only the women would do it.'

Mozambique's fifteen year experiment with Marxist socialism may have ended in November 1990, when the Mozambique Assembly voted unanimously to change its name from the People's Republic of Mozambique to the Republic of Mozambique, but the efforts of the Marxist Frelimo government have left their mark on the place of women in society.

There is a surprisingly high number of women in parliament, well over twenty per cent of seats are held by women. A much higher percentage than for Ireland, Britian, or the USA. But it is at the ground level that most of the work of rebuilding is being done. The old cooperative structures are still there; although some have shut down. The 'real politick' of international aid and World Bank loans doesn't have much time for inefficient cooperative farms, but the seeds planted in the minds of women during their first few years of independence have come back to life with the peace. Women tend to form automatically into work groups in the countryside where, like the building project at Gaza, the women have taken the initiative.

They make a strange sight singing traditional tunes in the windswept countryside just outside Maputo, where they work in second-hand clothes, woollen jumpers and headscarves. They sing in harmony as they make the concrete bricks for the £500 houses, and they are full of hope despite the dire economic conditions in the country. The difference now is that they see some way out after the misery of the war. A woman in a blue headscarf is happily, almost joyfully mixing the cement to haunting music and tunes. They are building for themselves, building their own homes and the hope shows.

More illustrative of the old-fashioned women of Mozambique is Eliza. According to the 'International Index of Human Suffering' published by the Population Crisis Committee in Washington (1992),[2] Mozambique is the unhappiest place on earth. It has an infant mortality rate of 161 per 1,000 live births,[3] and its annual income per capita for 1992 was $60, making it one of the poorest.[4]

Eliza Joao is typical of the poor illiterate peasant women whose lives have been set back another ten years by the poverty and lack of progress inflicted by the war. She has delivered nine children in her forty years.

78

Only six survived; two were still-born and a third died when the family hut collapsed on her. The latest baby, Isaura - eight months old - is wrapped in a red polka-dot shawl, popping up out of her mother's shawl like a mushroom in a white wool bonnet, and, despite the fact that Eliza looks completely exhausted and is living in dire poverty, she says simply: 'I like children.' Ask her about the family planning clinics that the agencies have tried to set up and she says in a conspiratorial whisper: 'some of the women don't know about it and a lot of the men don't like it. Some of the more modern families make two, three babies. The older families just go on the way they always did.' Ask her if her life is hard living in poverty in a barren landscape just outside Maputo, and she says: 'The living conditions are tough, we're hungry, life is hard now.'

At the heart of the women's movement in Mozambique is a woman who has done more than any other to raise awareness among women in Mozambique. Alcinda Abreu is the Minister for Social Welfare and led the country's delegation to Beijing in September; she is also a professor at the Centre for African Studies. She thinks that one of the main problems facing women following the war is the increase in the levels of domestic violence against women. Until the preparations for the Beijing conference began, it was very much a taboo subject, but, in the run up to Beijing and through the forums that met to prepare for the Fourth International Conference on Women, plans were made for the first home for battered wives in Maputo.

'During the first meeting people didn't speak out, but at the second meeting in June 1995, domestic violence was one of the major issues. There is much more domestic violence now, and it relates to the war. Women, children, and old people were the targets during the war. We have a lot of soldiers and children who were involved in the war, who are now demobilised, and we now have a culture of war and a culture of aggression. People cannot cope with economic problems. The soldiers are coming back home and can't go back to their original places; all these issues are contributing to a more violent society.'

This increase in domestic violence was behind the proposed creation of Mozambique's first battered wives shelter. At the meetings the women said that in most cases they were beaten frequently and because of the social stigma they never spoke out against it. Women like Eugina Vilunculos, who spent the civil war walking for miles everyday to keep safe, are fairly typical. 'Yes, he's given me a few slaps around the place and it has been worse since the war, but I don't bother with that kind of thing, it happens to everyone. All the men are under a lot of pressure because there is no jobs and not enough work.'

Abreu agrees: 'Women are always the first ones who have to resolve the problems, they have to find any survival strategy and this means they have to go out of the home and sometimes they bring back more money than the husband, and this creates very violent reactions from the side of the husbands.'

Economically, Mozambique has been destroyed by sixteen years of war which has left the vast potential of the country unrealised. The country is rich in gold, gems, and energy producing hydro-carbons, but when Mozambique finally won its independence from its Portuguese colonisers in 1975, the country had only one geologist and one mining engineer. The Frelimo government, which had led the fight for independence, tried to develop the mining potential, but the civil war drove away potential investors and expertise. However, in the last year alone the government has been approached by eighty-six foreign mining companies looking for permission to move into the country, and providing some hope of easing the dire unemployment situation. However, the Mozambique economy is so desperate to attract foreign investment that the government are taking in the mining companies on whatever terms the companies demand.

Another type of mine has left Mozambique with the war's most deadly legacy. In October the Mozambique government launched a major mine awareness project in the countryside. Many of the victims of the mines are rural women, who are mostly unaware of the dangers under their hoes as they try to till and prepare land after the war. So far in Mozambique, some 10,000 people have become mine victims. The Red Cross in Mozambique is at the forefront of a campaign launched in 1992 to ban the production of mines, which has so far led to their exports being halted by a number of European countries. For Eima, it is already too late.

Eima has been in a wheelchair for three years, since she lost her leg at Capizanje on the border between Mozambique and Malawi. She doesn't want to talk about it, but is eventually persuaded by the doctor at Maputo's central hospital, where five men in three workshops spend their days carving new wooden limbs for the victims. Eima lost her leg, but she also lost her husband after the accident. 'He met another woman and now he works in the mines in South Africa. He said I wasn't any use anymore.'

The doctor smiles more sympathetically and offers an explanation: 'out in the villages there's not much time for this love business. A woman can stay around for as long as she is useful for work and for the child, but once she gets on a bit or the children go away, she outlives her usefulness.' The doctor is apologetic about the brutal pragmatism forced onto them by poverty, but the country is also full of hope.

Carlos, a twenty-four year old mines victim limps across the exercise room on one crutch to talk about the mines he stepped on six months ago. He has only one leg but he smiles as he says: 'it's okay - I can still climb the mango tree' - an outlook that sums up Mozambique today, and especially its women, who seem to be doing most of the climbing.

NOTES:
1. Boothby, 1991, 'The Cost of Survival' published by USA Commitee for Refugees.
2. Population International, 1992.
3. UNICEF, 1996, The State of the World's Children. New York: Oxford University Press.
4. World Development Report, 1994. World Bank.

Focus on

Women and Rights in Mozambique

From 'The Situation of Women in Mozambique'
by Forum Mulher

In daily life women have fewer rights than men, even if they are equal before the law. It is clear that customary law continues to be practised in parallel with the laws laid down by the state, and here women do not have equal rights. The community courts, which are the legal authority to which most women apply, do not always apply the laws protecting women when judging a dispute, but follow customary norms placing women in an inferior position to men.

Although the Constitution enshrines the same rights for men and women, little was done to bring the existing norms into line with social change. Legal provisions that run counter to the proclaimed equality of rights are still in force, and are obstacles to change, preventing women from participating in the resolution of society's problems on an equal footing. The Assembly of the Republic, with the participation of civil society, is currently undertaking a review intended to bring the legislation into line with the new Constitution. The legislation in force enshrines inequality within the family by limiting women's legal and commercial capacity through marriage. This contrasts with the constitutional principles granting equal rights to men and women. The same law regulates relations between men and women in civil marriages by saying that administration of the couple's separate and common goods is the task of the man as head of family.

Mozambique has no family law separate from the Civil Code. The Draft Family Law has been in force since 1982, concretely the chapters dealing with de facto unions and divorce. With the introduction of the new Constitution in 1990, the Draft could no longer be used. The need to prepare a family law which is in harmony with the new Constitution and with the country's cultural characteristics is widely recognised.

Mozambique has two co-existing systems for rights to ownership and use of land - official law and, in parallel, customary law made up of a vast range of norms that vary from region to region. Their basic philosophies are contradictory (the law declares the land to be unalienable property of the state, while traditional norms consider it to belong to the community living on it and its ancestors), and the way in which each is applied continues to evolve in practice.

Women's access to, and rights over, land are badly documented in every statistic; detailed data on land ownership is very scarce, and is not disaggregated by sex. Though the Constitution grants men and women equal rights in access to land, women's rights are potentially weakened by marriage, particularly when in a regime of common goods, where the husband is presumed to be the manager of the family patrimony. Few land titles are allocated to women; as a rule, the man, as head of family, is the one who registers the ownership title.

In the case of single women, getting help to obtain a land title is a major problem.

The introduction of the Economic Rehabilitation Programme in 1987 led to reduced public expenditure on the social services such as health, education, social security, the withdrawal of subsidies on basic consumer items and currency devaluation, making women's lives even more difficult, since their access to income and services is reduced, and increasing amounts of their time are required to fill the gaps resulting from the real reduction in social services for the poorer population strata.

The range of actions of a social nature undertaken since independence, aimed at improving living conditions, could not be kept up, both for economic reasons and, more fundamentally, because of the destruction of socio-economic infrastructures during the war. In these circumstances, Mozambican families became poorer, the number of households headed by women increased, real purchasing power has been falling, and the pattern of the sexual division of labour throughout society remains unchanged.

In view of the principle of equal rights between men and women enshrined in the Mozambican Constitution, the OMM and later other organisations for women pressurised the government to ratify the *Convention for the Elimination of All Forms of Discrimination against Women*. This was done in 1993. However the importance of the event and the content of the Convention are not widely known, although some organisations are trying to develop initiatives to study its implementation and propose amendments to the Constitution and legislation currently in force.

The introduction of the *Law of Associations* in 1989, and the new Constitution of 1990, brought about major internal transformations with the freedom to form associations and a multi-party system. In this context, various associations and/or organisations in favour of women began to emerge, contributing to the struggle for improving the conditions of women.

In 1992, Forum Mulher was established, bringing together organisations and institutions working in favour of Mozambican women, namely national and foreign NGOs, state and research institutions, political party women's organisations, and national and foreign donors. The Forum's general objectives are the following:

• to form a network for communication, information and the exchange of experiences among everyone working on questions relating to women, gender, and development;

• to train people from the participating organisations and others, to, on the one hand, raise their level of knowledge about gender questions, and on the other make them more efficient in their work;

• to influence the decision-taking bodies on gender questions and the equality of rights and opportunities of access between women and men.

SOURCE: Forum Mulher's 'The Situation of Women In Mozambique', a report by the women's NGOs to the NGO Forum taking place concurrently with the African Preparatory Conference for Beijing in Dakar, Senegal.

After Conflict: Reconstructing Lives Against All the Odds

Róisín Boyd

The Philippines, Cambodia and Rwanda are countries which have been torn apart by terrible violence and injustice over the last twenty years. The thread common to all three is the demand for justice. This indicates the demand for recognition of crimes committed - the salvagings (disappearances), torture and murder of those trying to change their situation, feminists, trade-unionists, farmers - in the Philippines. There is also the demand for recognition of the genocide in Cambodia and of the genocide incited in Rwanda by the former government's death squads (the interhamwe).

In the Philippines, women were to the forefront of the struggle to overthrow the greedy and corrupt Marcos regime (supported for years by the USA). Ironically, many subsequently felt betrayed by a woman - President Cory Aquino. In Cambodia, the Khmer Rouge, in 1975 attempted to bring the country back to the year zero. The country had been so devastated under the puppet regime of Lon Nol - illegally bombed by the USA - that people thought the Khmer Rouge couldn't be any worse. But less than three years after the Khmer Rouge came to power, more than a million Cambodians were dead. The Khmer Rouge have never been brought to justice. In Rwanda, where again more than a million people suffered genocide, the survivors have not received justice.

I am going to tell you of some of the women I've met - women who refuse against enormous odds to give up their struggle for justice. What has struck me is the extraordinary courage of individual women. Their determination, against all odds, to find justice - not only for themselves but for their co-patriots, children and future generations. And despite everything, the ability to laugh and share their experiences so that others can know and maybe share and support their struggle to bring about change.

I went to the Philippines in 1986, just after Ferdinand Marcos had been overthrown by People Power bringing Cory Aquino to power. It was a time of great hope. Despite the enormous obstacles, people thought everything would improve. Of course Aquino was a widow - her husband Benigno had been assassinated on 21 August 1983. He'd said when he was alive that he pitied the leader who would follow Marcos. And there's no doubt that many now feel betrayed by Cory Aquino. The

85

looted wealth of the Marcos was of course notorious, indebting the Philippines to the tune of billions of dollars. Visiting their Malacanang Palace was a poignant, if bizarre, experience. Waiting in the queue to see Imelda's shoes, a woman, also waiting, explained how she felt saddened to see such wealth, knowing how poor the people were. There were two thrones with hearts inscribed with initials 'I' and 'F', their own dental clinic, and hundreds of empty boxes they'd obviously not had time to fill. The images were stark: the corruption of the Marcos, the purity and goodness of Aquino. But many were disillusioned with her as well. And in some ways this seemed worse. They'd hoped to rebuild their country after years of struggle, only to see their hopes dashed.

I visited Negros, where a large proportion of the Philippines' sugar is grown. As I flew in I was struck by the beauty of the green sugar cane glistening against the blue of the sea. But Negros is impoverished. Thousands of children suffer malnutrition. I met an extraordinary woman whom I called Therese. She didn't want me to use her real name, in 1986 because even though there'd been a change of power she wasn't sure how things would turn out. She was an organiser with the Federation of Sugar Workers. I stayed in her small house on stilts with its thatched roof. We spoke at night after she'd finished work, by the light of the oil lamp. Her electricity had been cut off by the landowner because of her trade union activities. Her 'co-workers', husband and children, sat around us as she explained her hopes for the future now that 'Cory' had come to power. They were hospitable, sharing what little they had - rice and tiny fish.

The next time I met 'Theresa' - in 1990 - she decided to use her real name which was Elma. I suppose she felt she'd been through so much in the meantime that using a false name was now meaningless. She had said in 1986 that 'when President Cory took over our government we felt hope, especially the poor people - that we will be uplifted from our poverty and that she [Cory] will implement land reform'.

But Elma's hopes were dashed. Elma had worked in feudal conditions, under which the plantation owner possessed not just the land but also his workers.

Elma would never forget 5 August 1987. She was woken by the military at 6.00 am. Twelve soldiers surrounded her house. 'They are calling my name'. 'What do you want, sir?' She asked them to wait while she got dressed. Meanwhile the commanding officer was shouting angrily, accusing her of being the district commander of the NPA (New People's Army - a communist guerilla group). She was brought to a military barracks, where she and her husband were questioned separately. She was punched and burnt with cigarettes, while they kept insisting she tell them her 'code-name' in the NPA. She was held for nine days. She didn't know what was happening to her children. Then she heard them on the radio appealing to know their mother's whereabouts. Elma's story is heartbreaking. She's a small woman, very thin, old, as

86

she says, at forty-nine. She had no change of clothes while she was imprisoned, and while telling her story she started to cry. 'I'd started to menstruate. I felt very bad because I did not change my clothes for nine days, and my monthly menstruation came. I have been suffering for my situation.'

On the ninth day, the officer said that they'd let her go but she'd have to go to the radio station first where there were questions and answers written out for her to read out. She was to say that she wasn't mistreated and to call on her co-workers to leave the union because she'd found out it was connected with the NPA. But Elma refused because, as she said, 'I know that the union isn't connected with the New People's Army. We have people who join the union because of the discontent and injustices they experience, but they are not members of the NPA'. After her broadcast, the telephone rang - it was her son, and there were international calls from supporters.

Most movingly, though, Elma described how on the forty-nine kilometre journey home she waved to people she knew, people she'd worked with. She was so terrified she'd be 'salvaged' - the term used in the Philippines for disappearances. 'I was showing the military that the people recognised me. I was thinking that if the military knew that plenty of people recognised me they would not kill me, so I kept waving my hands.' Elma continued: 'that was the experience I met with after one year of President Cory Aquino's government.'

Elma started to organise in 1976, 'Because I was born a sugar worker, and I experienced how hard it is to be a sugar worker'. She wanted to share her knowledge because very few of her colleagues had the chance to study.

After refusing to move from her house for years under the Marcos regime, Elma eventually had to leave and was moved to a new hacienda, which is where I met her the second time. She was moved as punishment for attempting to organise some redistribution of land, to make a co-operative. They were much worse off now because the land at the new hacienda was bad - nothing would grow. At least in the other hacienda she could grow and sell some vegetables. She showed me the dried land and her vegetables which in spite of tremendous effort, had simply withered.

She said, 'I have never experienced such hardship. I have only three children. When we were together [at the other hacienda] each night, the mothers tried to plan what we would do for tomorrow, and everyone said, "Oh God, I will sleep with my problem, and I will open my eyes tomorrow with the same problem"'.

After she'd been tortured, Elma stopped working for the Sugar Federation and started to work with the Catholic church. But, she said, 'On my part, I did not change. I want justice which is why I want to continue the struggle, because I have never, ever experienced justice'.

She explained how she couldn't sleep at night when there are military operations. 'I worry for my children. I am old, but I can still help with little things to continue the struggle for the people, so I do not want to die' and she laughed.

We left her off in the town where she was going to a meeting. I always remember seeing her small figure walking away. Her back straight. Determined. I hoped she'd be safe.

Visits to the Killing Fields

Cambodia is another country where the killers - the Khmer Rouge - were never punished. They actually held a 'government in exile' seat at the UN. The 'Coalition Government of Democratic Kampuchea' (CGDK) was the only 'government' recognised by the West. However, as Professor Ben Kiernan has pointed out, the CGDK was neither a coalition, nor a government, nor democratic.[1] The same amount of aid - some $300 million - was spent on the camps, controlled by the Khmer Rouge along the Thai border, as on the people in Cambodia. There were 300,000 refugees - 6.5 million people still in Cambodia. During the 1980s while aid continued at the camps, Cambodia was the only Third World country denied UN Development aid. It was being punished, as was Vietnam, because the United States lost the war against Vietnam.[2]

It's hard to imagine the impact of that denial of aid, and the West's refusal to acknowledge the genocide of more than a million people. When I first visited, the country was called Kampuchea. I was met by my guide, Chea, at the border. (I had travelled across from Vietnam, strangely enough in an old white Mercedes. I had wanted to get the bus, but the Vietnamese government guide wasn't having any of it). I was to see Kampuchea/Cambodia through her eyes for the next two weeks. It was difficult because information was very controlled. Chea, like all those still living in the country, had lived in horrendous conditions in the 'Pol Pot' labour camps - Khmers never referred to the Khmer Rouge but to Pol Pot. But as she said, she was 'lucky' she hadn't lost any close relatives - her parents had survived - but many aunts, uncles and grandparents had died. She was relatively privileged, I was to discover later. Her father was a government official, which was probably the reason she had the job as government guide.

The first places I was brought to were Choeng Ek and Tuol Sleng, both testimonies to what had taken place during the Khmer Rouge years in 1975-79. Tuol Sleng had been a school, but was turned into a torture chamber. Of the 20,000 people detained there for 'questioning', seven survived. I will never forget the photographs of the women, taken before they died (like the Nazis the Khmer Rouge documented their killing). Women with their children, women alone, men all staring out at the camera with terrified eyes, some trying to maintain some dignity, each with a number around their neck, or pinned to their clothes. All with the same hairstyle - everybody had to wear their hair in a 'bob' - and regulation black tunics. I asked Chea if she recognised anyone. She became upset and said she never looked at the photos because she was afraid she might.

Choeng Ek is a glass stupa (or monument) in which the pathetic bundles of rags and skulls of those killed are displayed. Shelves and shelves of skulls. I could hear children singing in a nearby school. I was always aware of the ghosts - all those thousands killed so cruelly in such a brutal manner. But people were getting on with their lives. They couldn't understand why they were still being punished. After the Vietnamese routed the Khmer Rouge in 1979, the West imposed an embargo on aid to Cambodia. They literally had nothing, except for the few NGOs that were there providing what they could - the only country in the world refused UN aid. Constantly, Cambodians asked me why they were being punished. Punished for surviving and for allowing the Vietnamese to rescue them from the Khmer Rouge. Many felt humiliated, as if they had to prove how much they'd suffered under the Khmer Rouge. As one old woman in the market said, 'if Satan himself had rescued us, we would have been grateful'.

Now, of course, women continue to suffer terribly - seeing their children die needlessly for lack of food and medicine; their husbands and sons being conscripted to fight the Khmer Rouge. Mines planted by the Khmer Rouge, and sometimes government forces, were and are the biggest problem Cambodia now faces. There are at least four million mines in Cambodia, and they are recognised as the biggest hindrance to development and reconstruction in the country. Thousands have lost their lives or limbs, and valuable land lies wasted, because it's mined. I visited Kompong Speu hospital, where all those who had lost a limb after stepping on a mine were being 'treated'. The hospital was almost bare - virtually no facilities. A young boy, sixteen years old, went to look for his cattle, stepped on a mine, and his leg and stomach were injured.

I met a woman lying on her bed in agony - the bottom part of her leg had been blown off. She'd been searching in the forest for firewood. What choice did she have? No firewood meant no fire to cook. She knew the risks she had to take to feed her family. On the way home with the wood, she stepped on a mine on the mountain road. She was twenty-four years old. She was in pain. It had happened twelve days ago. When I asked her if she was angry about those who'd planted the mine, she replied yes, she was angry with 'the Pol Pot men who put the mines on the road'. She was single. This would make it even more difficult for her because culturally, disabled women aren't seen as marriageable.

In Cambodia, as in other countries after conflict, there is a higher number of women than men - almost sixty per cent. Mostly widows and single women. I remember arguing with a member of Hun Sen's government one evening, as we sat outside. He was advocating polygamy as the answer, even though the government had voted against this 'solution', (under the Khmer Rouge, polygamy had been routine). He was amused and joked that it would be a great solution, and Cambodian men would love it. Of course, Cambodian women didn't like the idea at all. They resisted any attempts to bring it about.

I was brought to meet the Revolutionary Women's Association of Kampuchea (RWAK). The Association was against polygamy, and members felt stepfathers were not a good idea for the children from the first marriage. They said the double burden of Cambodian women was a result of the 'Pol Pot regime'. Many women had been widowed, and were left to raise their children alone.

The RWAK said their role was 'to arouse the women - the mass of women throughout the country and to serve the interest of women and children throughout the country'. They said there were women who had 'devoted' six or seven sons to the army. The official line in both Vietnam and Cambodia is that women always offer their husbands and sons to conflict willingly. In Cambodia, these women were faced with enormous obstacles. And they insisted that women's contribution be recognised. They cited a woman officer who'd been honoured for de-mining a field. They said women also played a role in persuading men to return from the Khmer Rouge. They went on radio to ask them to come home. Throughout my visit, I would hear the haunting voices of women and men over the radio begging people to come home.

The priorities of RWAK included educating women to increase their literacy, and educating men to help women with the housework, so women would have time to read the newspaper in the evening or listen to the radio! A lot of women would empathise with that, I'm sure.

I went back again for the elections in February 1993. Cambodia was, of course, very different. The embargo had been lifted, the Vietnamese had long gone and commerce was booming. New hotels, shops and businesses everywhere; the wide streets of Phnom Penh now full of trucks and cars - whereas before there had been bicycles and mopeds and motor bikes. The wonderful frangipani (prayer trees) with their scented white flowers still lined the streets. The UN had arrived to supervise the elections.

But there was of course a very unpleasant downside to all of this 'development', with women as the victims. Prostitution was everywhere; Khmer men used prostitutes as well, although this was an 'industry' catering principally for visitors.

I ended up in one of the 'men's bars' in Phnom Penh, with a group of Irish NGO workers, soldiers, gardai and a parliamentary group over for the elections whom I'd been interviewing earlier. I discovered women dressed in bikini type outfits of 'faux' animal skin. They'd come from the Philippines because the USA bases had closed at Clark and Subic in Olongopo, and they had no work. They were brought over for the duration of the elections by the American bar owner. One woman told me, quietly, from behind the bar, (she wasn't meant to talk), that they were kept as virtual slaves upstairs during the daytime.

While I was in Cambodia I discovered that there were many complaints from women UN staff about the behaviour of their male counterparts at the brothels and with the local and Filipino women. However, these women insisted that the only result of the complaints was that UN staff were ordered to keep their jeeps behind the brothels, so they wouldn't be visible.

The UN are long gone from Cambodia. They had their elections, but the problems remain - the Khmer Rouge still fight on. And mines remain the biggest problem. The new government have been accused of suppressing freedom of expression. Women are particularly strong in forging democratic organisations, and working for human rights. I went to look for Chea, my translator from earlier years. She had left. Gone to Holland where she'd married. We send each other Christmas cards. The last time she wrote, she told me her husband had lost his job. Chea, who'd always wanted to leave Cambodia for the West, had discovered it wasn't all it was cracked up to be.

Facing Genocide in Rwanda

On 6 April, 1994, a plane was shot down as it was returning to Rwanda. It was carrying the presidents of both Rwanda and Burundi, coming home, after signing a peace accord - the Arusha Agreement - in Tanzania. Twenty minutes later a brutal genocide began - unprecedented in Africa. It was calculated and cold-blooded. Not in any sense random. Probably at least a million Tutsis and moderate Hutus were murdered. What's unforgivable is that we in the West knew what was happening. The UN were there. Journalists were there. But the massacres were allowed to continue.

I went to Rwanda a year later. Inevitably, I approached a country with such a history with dread, remembering the terror I'd read about, the fear and the amazing courage of so many. On the plane was the usual collection of aid workers, evangelicals, missionaries and journalists. Rwandans were impatient with the number of aid agencies in their country - then more than 140 - many of whom had arrived a bit too late as far as they were concerned. Agencies were also criticised for competing for funds for the refugees - many of whom were suspected as responsible for the massacres during those terrible three months beginning in April. Ironically, these camps have received more aid than Rwanda itself or its government.

Rwanda was very different from what I'd been led to expect. There was an awful sense of a country peopled by ghosts. Many of the dead hadn't been buried, because their relatives wanted the 'evidence' to remain. The dead remained so that there could be justice, and so that the killers couldn't deny what had happened. This was a constant refrain - justice. Not revenge. Justice. But people were carrying on with their lives. The government of the RPF (Rwandan People's Front), were trying to run the country with very little, and to prevent retaliation by the survivors. But with very little support.

Rwanda is a beautiful country. Everywhere there is greenery, bougainvillaea, sweet smelling flowers and birds singing. How incongruous it seemed to be, walking on the streets of Kigali admiring the trees and enjoying the climate. Of course I could never forget the thousands who only a few months earlier had been hacked to death. Always the deep sadness as I listened to the stories, from child after child, of how they'd been attacked: the machete wounds still visible on their heads: the roads bristling with aid vehicles - government ministers travelling by bike - and the Mille Colline hotel open for business again, and booked out; the pool glistening in the sun; Rwandans stooping to pick weeds out of the lawns while the expats enjoyed the sun. A note in the hotel rooms apologised to guests that they couldn't yet provide room service. In this very hotel only months earlier, the brave manager had tried to rescue people, as Rakiya Omaar, a lawyer and member of African Rights, reports in her extraordinary testimony - 'Death, Despair and Defiance'.

I met Rakiya in Kigali at the hotel. She's an exceptional woman who has been driven to record what really happened in Rwanda, and she's angry that the truth is now being distorted, that the survivors are being ignored. She has recorded how church and state collaborated in the genocide. Rakiya was tired - exhausted by hearing testimony after testimony. But she was determined to continue. She firmly believed that a new society could not be created until justice was seen to be done. Until the leaders of the genocide, in Kenya, Zaire, France, Canada and elsewhere were tried. Painstakingly, she'd spoken to hundreds of witnesses, and recorded the unthinkable - neighbours killing neighbours, women participating in killing, and priests standing at checkpoints targeting those to be killed.

The next time I spoke to Rakiya, by telephone, she was back in London, and she said: 'you won't like my next report, "Not so Innocent, When Women Become Killers"'. I suppose she felt that as a feminist I'd find it hard to accept. She told me later that some women at the Beijing Conference didn't think it was appropriate to highlight women's involvement in the genocide. But of course we have to know what really happened, and we can't choose to highlight women's role in history only when it's positive.

Apparently, many of the women named in the report are still working in Rwanda or living abroad, in Europe or Africa, some in the refugee camps. The report stresses why it is important to expose women's participation: 'failure to do so reinforces the impunity that is enjoyed by the genocidal criminals.'[3] There were of course many heroic Hutus, women and men who risked their own lives to save their Tutsi friends and neighbours. Those rebuilding Rwanda want everyone to identify as Rwandan rather than Tutsi, Hutu or Twa; to do away with 'ethnicity' - discarding the identity cards (introduced by the Belgians) which the former regime had used to such effect to wipe out the Tutsis.

I met Yvonne (which is not her real name as she was still too frightened to use her own), who is a teacher at a centre for children. Like so many, she was extremely dignified, calm and almost matter of fact when telling me her story. She, a Tutsi, had hidden in the roof of a Hutu friend's house for those terrible few months. Never knowing when the 'interhamwe' (death squads) would come for her. She had been politically active in a teacher's union, in the preceding years. A very courageous activity, given that her colleagues and friends had already been targeted and murdered. No opposition to the Habyarimana regime had been tolerated. She told me she had feared something terrible would happen on the scale it did. Now she was working with children - the new generation - and she hoped for a better future. Like everyone I spoke to, she believed there could be no peaceful future without justice first. Justice had to be seen to be done.

I met Veneranda Nzambazamariya at what had been a thriving women's centre. Now it was a shell - the white-washed walls pockmarked by shells; all their files, built up painstakingly over the years, destroyed. But Reseau des Femmes, the network of women, were determined to rebuild their centre. Already they were holding their meetings in bare rooms - rooms without any furniture. They were sad but not grim, determined to go on. Veneranda, a tall, striking woman in a bright pink blouse, says women have to be involved in Rwanda's reconstruction so that 'there can never be another genocide in Rwanda'. She wants women to play a key role in reconstruction, rehabilitation and reconciliation. 'But didn't women take part in the massacres?', I ask Veneranda. She agrees that women did indeed take part but says 'if we have action for peace, if women stand up as one to say "stop", we can stop that violence!' And she believes that it's important that women have a key role in education, to 'give children new values'.

Veneranda had fled the country as the genocide began. But like so many Tutsis and moderate Hutus, she'd lost 'an aunt, uncles, cousins and good friends'. Her voice falters, but as we stand beside the women's centre, she points to the flowers growing profusely on the wall. 'When I came back, I was so sad but I told myself life has to continue, the sun is shining, look at those beautiful flowers. You know, you see the houses completely destroyed, but behind them the flowers are very beautiful. I ask myself, 'how is it possible?' Humans are cruel but nature is generous. So maybe there is hope. We have to continue to live. And we have to live completely: if not, you are dead. I decided to live and start again our women's organisation.'

Veneranda's optimism was authentic, and many women in Rwanda were looking to the future. But some women, like Clare, seemed bereft of hope. On 3 June 1994 her husband and little daughter had been taken out of the house by Hutu neighbours. For their own protection, she was told. Clare never saw them again. She hid for months with their two month old baby - terrified she might be discovered. At night, they hid under the broad leaves of pumpkin bushes. She laughed, not a joyful sound, but with embarrassment and humiliation at the memory of it, when she described how she and others would imitate a dog's bark if they heard the interhamwe. 'Then they'd think it was a dog eating a dead body.' Clare now works for an NGO. Her pain was so acute I wondered how she survived. She told me of her belief in God and the hope of meeting her loved ones in heaven. And now, a widow, like thousands of others in Rwanda, she had to support her family.

Angeline Ledekubana fled Rwanda in 1963, when she was five. Her father had been killed earlier in one of the pogroms against the Tutsis. Now back in Kigali, she works for an NGO. Her sister is a government minister, who fought with the RPA, and now fights different battles to rebuild the country. Angeline says she thinks 'there is a reconciliation process, but that cannot happen as quickly as some people think, particularly the foreigners. They think it's a mechanical process. That you call people "come and reconciliate" and then we'll give you money. But it's not like that. It's a reality we've lived through this; it's a reality we have to accept that people have been hurt, and that others have been transformed into some kind of animals. To be able to massacre or kill your own wife, just because she's different, or you've been told by someone to do it. Then you need another process that takes much longer. Life has to go on. We are trying now to rebuild classrooms, and water systems and people have to cultivate, have to go back to their homes. Those who survived need shelter. They need to form their communities which are very difficult to form. If you take people like me who grew up in different countries, and come back with a different culture and attitude than my colleagues who grew up here ... to form us into a cohesive community again will take a lot of energy. It's part of cooling down the minds of the people. And you can't have a reconciliation without justice'.

NOTES:
1. Davies, P and Dunlop, N *War of the Mines*, Pluto, London, 1994.
2. Mysliwiec, Eva *Kampuchea Punishing the Poor*, Oxfam, Oxford 1988.
3. Africa Rights, *Not So Innocent, When Women Become Killers*, African Rights, London, 1995.

Focus on

Fighting Back in Sri Lanka

Geraldine Terry

Every so often we're reminded of Sri Lanka's twelve-year civil war between government forces and the Liberation Tigers of Tamil Eelam (LTTE) or 'Tamil Tigers'. Whenever fighting intensifies or another suicide bomber strikes, it is back in the headlines. An estimated 50,000 people have been killed in that war, mostly in the north and east, while military activity and terror tactics have forced hundreds of thousands to flee their homes. During that period the south of the country has not been immune from large-scale violence, but not so many of us have heard anything about the political troubles which wrecked the south between 1987 and 1990. The completely separate conflict ended with an estimated 17,000 dead or 'missing'.

These bald statistics of deaths and ruined lives subsume the individual stories of thousands of men, women and children from Sri Lanka's main communities - the majority Sinhalese - the Tamils and the Muslims. Many of the victims are women, something it is easy to forget. Women who have been shot at or shelled. Women who have been attacked by mobs in the street. Women who have been herded onto buses and driven from their homes in Tamil Tiger 'ethnic cleansing' operations. Women who have seen their husbands dragged out and shot at midnight.

Everyone in this part of the country has suffered in some way from the LTTE-government conflict. On a recent trip to the village of Kinnaya, I met S Vallipallai, a small, frail woman in her early seventies. When, in 1990, the army and LTTE were fighting for control of Trincomalee and its surrounds, the entire Tamil population of Kinnaya - about 1,500 people - fled into the jungle and hid. With the battle raging around them, they stayed there for six days without food or water.

'It was the rainy season, so everything was soaked. We dug shallow pits and drank the water that collected in them. We drank water which had collected in animal footprints in the ground, and from ponds where elephants and cattle had urinated. Some people had managed to bring a bit of rice, others some salt. Otherwise we had nothing for us or the children to eat except for coconuts from the trees. Sometimes helicopter gunships hovered overhead, firing into the bush. I needed to change my clothes, as in my terror I had run away with only what I had on my back. So I decided to risk slipping back into Kinnaya. Me and three other women set off. I had to take my granddaughter, just a little girl then. When we got to the village we saw there were soldiers everywhere. They were standing around watching our Muslim neighbours looting our houses. A Home Guard man saw us and threw a rock at me - it hit me on the upper back. Then he ran over and hit me with his rifle butt. I tried to run off but he caught me. He punched me and pushed me into a pond, shouting and screaming "I bet your son's a Tiger!" But none of my family have ever had anything to do with the Tamil Tigers. Then the most frightening thing happened; he lined us all up and was just raising his rifle when some army officers saw what was happening and shouted at him to stop. We escaped back into the jungle - but still with no clean clothes. I was badly hurt, but of course it was impossible to get any treatment. A few days later we all came out of the jungle. We just couldn't stand it any more, what with the helicopters and the gunfire. And a teacher in the village told us that the army were going to start shelling LTTE positions in the jungle, so we had better get out.'

And now? Vallipallai's troubles are not over yet. The trauma of those days in the jungle and her victimisation by the Home Guard man has left her with panic attacks and breathing difficulties. Twice she has had to go into hospital. For five years after being forced out of Kinnaya she and the other Tamil inhabitants lived in a 'camp' in old World War Two aircraft hangars in Trincomalee. But in July 1995 all the camp-dwellers were evicted by the army, who said they needed the base. Thirty-five families went back to Kinnaya, but not to their own land. In their absence, Muslim families had commandeered it. When I last saw her, Vallipallai was living in a temporary hut on a barren patch of somebody else's land, waiting for the result of a legal case which she hoped would end in the land being returned. After only a couple of days, she and her daughter had already set up a tiny shop. And that's how I remember her - a neat, white-haired woman standing in her shop selling sweets to a bunch of children; a picture of resourcefulness in adversity.

Pakistan: Women's Rights and Roles

Aileen O'Meara

'Catholicism and Islamic fundamentalism have a lot in common,' commented Hina Jilani, a human rights lawyer, in her office in Lahore, when I told her where I was from. 'I met your president Mary Robinson in Strasbourg some years back at a human rights conference, and we compared constitutions. In fact our constitution is far more liberal than yours!' Despite the differing geography and culture, Ireland and Pakistan have a lot in common.

The Setting

As we discussed Ireland's forthcoming divorce referendum in the crowded office of her legal aid practice, Hina pointed out that under the Pakistani constitution, all citizens are equal before the law. It is the so-called Islamicisation of the laws that has compromised the secular spirit of their constitution. Divorce and contraception are allowed under the secular constitution, although abortion, while it isn't mentioned in the constitution, is in effect illegal in Pakistan.

One could easily see how the Jilani-Robinson conversation could have gone. The two human rights lawyers might have discussed male dominated legislatures; the history of social opposition to married women's involvement in the workforce - memories of how women did not drink openly in Irish public houses, but were instead consigned to the 'snugs'; how married women lost their jobs, and found discrimination at many levels.

There are many similarities in the two countries' adoption of a majority religion in its public life - calls to prayer over loudspeakers or from national radio, prayers in schools and in parliaments, and an intolerance by the religious fundamentalists of minority religions and belief in a secular state.

Pakistan is a male dominated society, signalled in its culture and dress codes, and the invisibility of women at many levels of social life. Women are kept inside. If they travel outdoors, it is frowned upon to be alone, and you do not see women smiling on the street.

Sons get preference in the family. Girl children often get no education; women are not treated as equal - they are for bearing children and doing housework. In poorer areas, they have little access to health care, and to economic independence. Even some of those who work outside the home hand over all of their wages to their husband or mother-in-law.

The following facts give an indication of the position of women in Pakistan, which is a patriarchal society despite its female Prime Minister, Benazir Bhutto:

• Female literacy is 24.7 per cent, and less than ten per cent in the villages;
• Life expectancy of Pakistani women is among the lowest in the world at 58.3 years;
• The female-male ratio is ninety-one women to 100 men - among the lowest in the world, this compares with a ratio of ninety-nine women to 100 men for Ireland;
• Almost ninety per cent of lactating women are anaemic (UNDP, 1994).

Domestic violence is widespread in Pakistan, and as elsewhere, while the laws recognise incest, rape, marital rape, and wife battering as criminal offences, the police are inclined to treat these issues as domestic matters rather than police affairs. In these cases the way forward lies not so much in law reform as with drastic changes in social attitudes.

Violence against women includes stove burning - a practice where women are pushed into open fires or stoves and their injuries are then attributed to their own carelessness - kidnapping, gang rape, and murder. Because women, in tribal communities in particular, are seen as possessions to be bought and sold, they have few rights within the family or community.

Women have few property rights. Although Islam prides itself on the fact that it gives women property rights that are specifically laid down, in fact many women in Pakistan do not actually get the inherited property that they are entitled to, especially if it is in the form of rural farm-land.

Bonded labour also exists amongst the lowest income groups and affects men, women, and children. In agriculture women and children work an average eighteen hours a day.

In Pakistan, as in Ireland, feminists have been to the fore in the human rights movement, campaigning for equality of opportunity and equal status at all levels in societies where traditional attitudes and practices weighed heavily against the females.

For Irish women, there have been some significant changes in recent decades, and the control and influence of the Roman Catholic church on their lives is rapidly diminishing. In Pakistan, the opposite seems to have happened, with the fundamentalists coming to the fore since 1977 under the protection of martial law. This has led to an oppressive and dangerous attitude towards women who do not abide by the strict and legal codes of what is perceived as Islamic law, particularly amongst the poor and lower middle classes.

According to the proponents of an Islamic state, it is on the women's morality that all social stability rests. Woman, state and Islam are all interlinked, and it is the women who is supposed to shoulder the burden of society's stability.

Emerging from Martial Law

The years of martial law ran from 1977 to 1985. During this time General Zia-ul Haq created a climate of fear and left a series of laws and ordinances that have reversed much of the progress made for and by women, increased conservatism, and in some cases created more oppression. This, reinforcing customs dating back to feudal times, has further frustrated women's potential in this South Asian country.

According to the Women's Action Forum in Pakistan 'although martial law was technically lifted in 1985, and parliamentary democracy restored in 1988, this last decade gives evidence to the reluctance of state and patriarchal powers to relinquish social, legal, and economic control.

'Many of the discriminatory laws are still on the statute books and while there is space now to express the concerns of women more freely, many of the retrogressive and detrimental forces unleashed by the military regime continue to destroy the very fabric of Pakistani society'.

Despite the fact that religious parties hold just six seats in Parliament, and have received only three per cent of electoral support, they have huge street power and the religious lobby is very potent. They also run schools, teaching fundamentalism to low income male children.

Islamicisation of the laws of Pakistan dates back to 1979 and the introduction of General Zia-ul-Haq's series of ordinances. These include The Hudood Ordinances (1979) which covered extra-marital sex (zina) and rape. It is worth mentioning that this law was passed against the recommendation of the then Shariat bench of religious scholars. The Shariat bench was dismissed by government for opposing stoning which they believed not to be a Quaranic punishment, and a new bench subsequently passed the law which the government wanted.

Among other things the law prescribes 100 lashes and, under certain conditions, stoning to death for adultery. Under this law, to prosecute a rape case, a woman needs the testimony of four adult Muslim male witnesses as proof that the crime had taken place. This makes it virtually impossible to prosecute a rape. A woman who registers a case of rape can, by her own admission, be prosecuted for adultery while a rapist goes free for lack of evidence. According to the Human Rights Commission of Pakistan (HRCP), over eighty per cent of women in jail in Pakistan today have been arrested for zina.

The Law of Evidence (1984) stipulates that in financial obligations (when reduced to writing) the testimony of two men or one man and two women is required. The law renders a woman's testimony in financial matters as legally half that of a man's, except when she signs in an official capacity, such as that of a bank officer.

The Qisas and Diyat (retribution and blood money) Ordinance (1990) introduced the concept of retribution on the basis of an eye for an eye; it allows murderers to pay blood money in lieu of punishment if the victim's family so agrees. Qisas and Diyat fixes the price of a human life in economic terms, based on whether the murdered person is a bread winner, what he or she would bring home every month - in essence, what has been the economic loss to the family. It consequently leads to the economic value of a woman being put at less than that of a man. It also leads to the problem that it is easier for a rich man to kill a poor man since he could afford to pay the blood money.

In 1986 The Pakistan Penal Code was amended so that any verbal or non-verbal, written or oral act can, by imputation, insinuation, or implication be interpreted as blasphemous, carrying an obligatory death sentence. Commonly known as the blasphemy laws, these sections undermine the basic tenets of human rights and have been used to victimize people. According to the HRCP, there were over 500 cases registered under the blasphemy laws in 1994, for which sections carry the mandatory death penalty. Charges include pretending to be a Muslim, use of Islamic terminology by non-Muslims, insulting the religion or the Prophet, or burning the holy Quran.

Under General Zia a parallel court system known as the Shariat Court System, was established. These courts examine every law to bring it into conformity with the Shariat; the 1991 Shariat Act provides for the supremacy of the Shariah. A Council of Islamic Idealogy was established as a consultative body by Zia, and used to re-examine the constitution with a view to removing laws repugnant to Islam and adding pro-Islamic legislation.

The Women's Action Forum claims that this council 'has been responsible for tabling some of the most damaging anti-women laws and policies between 1979 and 1991'.

Purdah

One of the most striking things about Pakistan is the clothing. On the one hand there is a tremendous variety of colour and styles. Women wear saris, men and women wear shalmar-qameez (a long shirt and loose trousers) in slightly different styles, and men and women both wear dhotis (a sarong with a split in the middle which shows both legs, and which is worn in the riverine areas where people have to hitch up their clothes to cross the river). One of the special pleasures of Pakistani women seems to be their beautiful clothes, and even the poorest women wear beautiful clothes since they embroider them elaborately for themselves, and therefore they do not cost very much. Everything is in the brightest colours and even the all enveloping burqa (a massive veil) is often made of bright oranges and pinks or black lacework.

To the West, it is the dress code - the chador, or burqa and the prevalence of the system of purdah - that is seen as most oppressive to women, although in Pakistan less than half the women wear any kind of chador or purdah.

The 'oppression' of the purdah is not so straightforward on the ground, according to Dr Farzana Bari, head of the Department of Women's Studies in the University of Islamabad. 'Those who are born into it do not necessarily see the purdah as a system of oppression. The chador protects them against harassment on the street. It also gives them privacy. But few would choose to wear it. I don't wear it, and my sister has been negotiating with her husband for years to drop it.'

Purdah is mostly practised in lower middle class and middle class families. Educated women rarely practise it, and poor women must leave the home to work, so they have no choice. Purdah is also a regional practice: there are great differences between the North West Frontier province, for example, and the Punjab province. In the latter, it is rare to see the full chador worn by women. It is much more strictly enforced in the North West Frontier province.

Statistically in the country as a whole, fewer than thirty per cent of the women cover their face. 'The veil signifies segregation,' said Dr Bari, 'and there is little segregation in the poor rural areas, where women work in the fields and on the roads. But the veil determines women's overall social and economic role in society.'

However, according to Dr Bari 'there is also a very specific dress code. A woman must look modest at all times, and if you are looking around on the street, you might be seen by men as a loose woman. You are more vulnerable without the veil, people can hassle you'.

She feels that men have a dual attitude to women in Pakistan. 'On the one hand they patronise women, attack them physically, pinch them in public places. Men also protect them, they believe that women need protection. There is the attitude that young women are dangerous, and must be kept inside. It is dual thinking.'

The Forces of Change in Pakistan: the Human Rights Campaigners
'The law is used in this country to maintain the status quo, therefore it is an instrument of suppression, especially against women,' said Hina Jilani, in Lahore. Together with her sister, Asma Jahangir, she has fought since the days of the Zia regime against human rights abuses and the use of the Hudood Ordinances.

The sisters have campaigned on human rights issues since they were teenagers, when their father was arrested for challenging the military regime. Both mastered in Law and opened an all-woman practice, where most of their clients are women.

Asma was arrested for sedition under the Zia regime, and both have received death threats from opponents of their human rights work. Asma won prestigious awards for her defence of a fourteen-year-old boy and his uncle in a blasphemy case. She received death threats and came under criticism for her stance.

Despite these laws, Hina is adamant that the country is essentially a secular one. 'We are not a fundamentalist Muslim country. No more than twenty per cent of people are practising Muslims, though the dominant elite, a small class, have a strong vested interest in retaining the status quo. Pakistan is a feudal society; all our institutions including the judiciary reflect feudal ideas.'

Hina Jilani and her sister fight daily battles in courts and prisons for women, against these laws on rape, adultery, and domestic violence. While their aim is to have the laws revoked, she does not believe that this is possible at present under the Bhutto regime, because of the power of the religious parties and their ability to organise massive street demonstrations, which the opposition would use.

The energy behind the human rights work in Pakistan is almost tangible. As Hina describes it: 'our campaigns are not just writing letters, holding press conferences or using the courts. Every day there are protest marches for women's issues; we have been in rallies several times on issues. You have to take risks. I mean that in the sense that one has to take a risk as a lawyer and go out in the streets against a judgement of the court. Even when you have got the law made, you can't sit back. Then you have to start monitoring how the law is being implemented and how it is not being implemented.' Rather than seeking to interpret Islamic law ('there are seventy-two different religious sects, all with different interpretations of the same source - the Quran') in legal cases, the team use the international standards of equality in their arguments. 'We look to society's practices that have a positive effect, and to the world community, to formulate certain standards. Once you accept that all human beings are equal, whatever their sex or religion, that is a universal standard.'

For Hina, the negative impact of the laws on women can be seen in the jails. When she started practising in the Seventies, there were only ten to fifteen women in jails. Since then the female prison population has risen dramatically. The vast majority are there under the Hudood Ordinances. 'The criminal justice process is brutal. Custodial violence is very common. Women who go to police stations are often beaten or raped there.' A prison survey was conducted in the Punjab province, which showed that seventy per cent of women were subjected to some form of violence, including rape or beatings.

'Our society is very traditional,' says Nazreen Azhar, of the HRCP. 'It happens everywhere that men want to control who women marry, and how they lead their lives.'

'Society maintains that religion gives women a high status,' said Nasira Habib, director of the Lahore-based Khoj, the research and development centre, 'but our societal norms and our social traditions, which go back centuries, don't give equality to women.'

'Poverty is the greatest hindrance to change in rural areas,' says Nazreen Azhar. 'The social customs are brutal towards women. Take "karo kari", for example, in the Sind province, where if a woman and man marry without their parents' consent, they can both be killed, and sometimes are.'

Artists and Activists

Tehreema Mitha is a rarity in Pakistan, a trained classical dancer. Rare, because dance was banned under Zia, and it is still very difficult to perform publicly, or advertise her performances. She dances before mixed audiences, mostly invited or carefully chosen. Now, for the first time in twenty years, a Pakistani-wide festival with Tehreema and other classical dancers is being held open to the public.

Yet while the potential of the rich cultural life of Pakistan - in its music and dance - is beginning to be publicised again, Tehreema's life is full of risks.

Classical dance has never been presented to the masses in Pakistan. After General Zia took over, the only dancing that was allowed, albeit clandestinely, was dancing by prostitutes, and so over the last two decades, dancing has become linked in the minds of many Pakistanis to prostitution. To dance at a public performance, Tehreema must get a NOC - No Objection Certificate - from the Ministry of Culture, allowing her to do 'movement and mime', promising that she will not engage in 'dance or other obscenities'. Tehreema must be careful about her newer dances. For example it is not possible to show anything explicitly sexual.

'You can feel unsafe and insecure all the time,' she said. 'My protection comes from the knowledge that my father is well-known, and that my husband comes from a certain strata of society. I have nothing that comes from me that gives me security.' Being a dancer makes her feel physically unsafe, mainly because she is promoting modern dance, which is new to her audience. 'With every new dance, I worry a little.'

Kishwar Naheed had been working in the civil service when Zia took over. 'They couldn't throw me out, but they put me in the back office.' The police followed her for three years. But it didn't stop her. An outspoken and fearless critic of the dictator, she writes poetry that captures the attitudes towards women in this patriarchal society. From 'We Sinful Women':

> *It is we sinful women who come out raising the banner of truth*
> *up against the barricades of lies on the highways*
> *who find stories of persecution piled on each threshold*
> *who find the tongues which could speak have been severed.*

Kishwar says that many countries, not just Pakistan, have blasphemy laws, and, like many intellectuals, is careful to point out that while campaigning for equality and human rights, Pakistanis do not want Western values imposed upon their culture. 'People here are secular, they are progressive, reasonable, and humanitarian. I can travel to the north-western part of this country and find an old woman educating a girl to be a nurse, or find an educated woman opening a school.'

Indeed, many activists were quick to point out that the West cannot escape the part it played in the retrogressive policies and actions of the military government in Pakistan.

Uzma Pirzada runs a literacy project in Lahore for young girls. 'I'm a devout Muslim, I pray five times a day, prayer is important in my life,' she said, while pointing out that she does not wear a veil. Educated and from a middle class background, she feels Islam is important in society. 'Spirituality is important for people, they do not see Islam as oppressive to them.'

The NGOs

Pattan is a non-governmental organisation established in the rural Punjab region after floods washed away thousands of homes in 1992. From an emergency basis in the beginning, the NGO now works to empower and enable the villagers in the riverine region to help themselves improve their lives from a situation of dire poverty and illiteracy. In Shapur village the women's group is opinionated and aware of their needs; despite almost 100 per cent illiteracy, they want their girl children educated and improvements in sanitation.

When funding the rebuilding of destroyed villages, Pattan insisted that men and women have dual ownership. 'This has had a huge impact,' said Sarwar Bari of Pattan. 'It has made women feel much stronger, and it changed the men's attitudes. Women were more confident in standing up to their husbands, and the men respected the women more. They see ownership and literacy as huge steps towards bettering their lives.'

In Peshawar, in the North West Frontier province, Maryam Bibi runs Khwendo Kor, a woman's centre teaching literacy and environmental education, and running a savings scheme and income generation projects in the outlying villages. Female literacy in the NWFP is less than 6.5 per cent and less than a third of schools teach girls. Here, purdah is strictly enforced and girls rarely travel far. 'Many need their children for working and home, and don't see the point in having them educated,' said Maryam.

On a visit to Telaband village outside Peshwar, women met others from nearby villages to hear about their income generation projects. Non-formal training is used by NGOs in this region, where no schools exist for girls.

Female district education officers employed by NGOs travel to villages, and venture into households where strict purdah is observed, and encourage women to educate their daughters, by pointing out that educating their daughters will help solve their health problems. Schools have been opened in villages where no government schools exist, and if there is an educated woman in the village, she is paid to run the classes in the mornings; there are no fees or uniforms, and books are provided.

Despite different situations, the poorer women in Baghbanpura, the urban slum on the edge of Lahore city are also concerned about education and sanitation, and the group of twelve enthusiastic women in a small room above their street had just finished writing a paragraph about their home on the day I visited.

'The women can now speak Urdu which is the common language of the country, rather than their own dialect,' said Sabiha Shabeen, adult education project officer with Khoj, the NGO running the project. 'The benefits are in confidence and manners, in being able to write a letter. The women can now manage their finances better, are more aware of the world and are teaching their children.'

Shabnam is in her late teens. 'My parents don't think I need to read and write, because my job is to cook and care for my family. But I want to know about the world. Before I was afraid of educated people, but now I can understand Urdu and speak with the people.'

The Future

Women's groups point to some positive signs for the future of Pakistan. The establishment of women's police stations has been an important step in the right direction; the Women's Bank, staffed by women and giving loans to women, has been another significant step in helping many women establish their own incomes. The Pakistani government has also signed CEDAW - the Convention on the Elimination of All Forms of Discrimination Against Women - an indication of its intention to work to guarantee equal rights for women. Finally in her previous government, Benazir Bhutto established a committee to look at the reform, though not the repeal, of the Hudood Ordinances.

Activists continue their work tirelessly. 'We are trying to break down doors that were previously closed to women,' said Shekla Zia, from Aurat, a resource and development centre for women, based in Islamabad. But she is not optimistic about the repeal of the laws against women. 'There is just such extreme reluctance at political level to touch things that the religious parties have an involvement in. The political pressure is not there, women's rights issues don't figure in their list of priorities.'

Kishwar Naheed is hopeful: 'Of course I have hope for the future. Women have been emerging over the past ten years, they are getting the top places in our colleges. They are the hope for change in Pakistan.'

BIBLIOGRAPHY:
Women's Action Forum (1995), 'Struggle for Women's Rights in Pakistan',
    Pakistan. (summary for Beijing).
UNDP, (1994), 'Human Development Report 1994', New York: Open University
    Press.

Traditionally excluded from obtaining credit from banks and other formal lending agencies, low-income rural women are benefiting from the establishment of small independent savings and loan schemes. Pictured above is Rubuia of the Pakistani NGO Pattan, with members of the Sunaki village women's saving/loan scheme. (Pakistan: Women's Rights and Roles by Aileen O'Meara)

Photograph by Liz Clayton.

Communities in Development:
the Theory and Practice of Gender

Mary Jennings

Many of the chapters in this book vividly describe the lives of women in various parts of the world and how economic policies, laws, customs, war and disease impact on women differently from men. Understanding these differences and their underlying causes forms the basis of a gender analysis. Much has been written over the past two and a half decades on the situation of women worldwide, yet, despite three earlier conferences on women (Mexico 1975, Copenhagen 1980 and Nairobi 1985), the conclusion at the start of the Fourth World Conference on Women in Beijing (FWCW) (September 1995) was that the situation of women had worsened, particularly in the economic and political fields. Why is this so? Clearly, there are no easy answers and the process of change is slow and complex. However, what has become apparent over the decades is that focusing on women only will not yield solutions, but that the relations between men and women and their influence on development must be understood and addressed.

The FWCW was a landmark in terms of recognition of progress along the road to full equality between women and men. The Programme of Action and the Declaration adopted commit the participants - 189 countries and the European Union - to taking action on many discriminatory issues confronting women. In particular, there was an acknowledgement that women's rights are human rights; that violence against women is not acceptable; there was considerable focus on equality for the girl child and a condemnation of genetic selection of the sex of foetuses and selective abortion; progress on inheritance rights for women was achieved; there was agreement that rape in time of war will now be regarded as a war crime; and for the first time, a commitment to recognition of women's non-remunerated work. Governments were called upon to ratify the Convention on ending discrimination against women; to revise their legislation irrespective of customary rules and legal practices; and to take the necessary steps to enable women to participate in all aspects of decision-making at political, economic, social, cultural and environmental fields, and in the fight against poverty.[1]

In discussing the development approaches to women that have been adopted over the last four decades and the shift from women-in-development to gender and development, this chapter provides a context to understanding the background to many of the FWCW issues. It considers the impact on women of being perceived initially only as mothers, and later, only as producers. It provides an understanding of gender and with examples from a range of countries it illustrates how women are discriminated against by law with regard to marriage, divorce, inheritance, and in the labour market. It examines the policies of donors towards mainstreaming WID (Women in Development) into existing policies and structures and the contrasting call by women, especially in the South, for the need to transform the current development agenda. It discusses the failure of projects to meet even their own WID/gender objectives, and the limitations of individual projects to affect transformation. No easy recipes for gender-aware policy formulation and planning are available: attitudinal and behavioural change is a slow process, but development players are urged to support the organisation of women so that Southern women can analyse their own societies, cultures, and economies, and determine the way forward themselves.

Women in Development (WID): from Mothers to Producers

From the 1950s until the early 1970s, it was assumed that with modernisation and economic growth, living conditions and wages would improve, and the benefits of economic growth would 'trickle down' to all segments of society. An examination of the impact of early development projects and programmes during this time revealed that women were not benefiting, and indeed, that many projects may have had a negative impact on them. In agriculture, for example, as new technologies were introduced, they were targeted at men despite the fact that in Africa women are the primary food producers. No recognition was given to women's economic and political needs, nor to the reality of their lives where they were an integral part of the development process, and change, taking place. The first approach to 'women in development' manifested itself in welfare projects such as nutrition, hygiene, and maternal and child health. During this period, women were largely invisible to development planners except in their roles as mothers.

In the 1970s, there was a recognition that rapid economic growth could not take place in developing countries because of the social bottlenecks which prevailed. Thus, there was a shift from a preoccupation with economic growth to an emphasis on meeting people's basic needs and addressing the 'poorest of the poor'. Low income women, but especially female-headed households, were seen as being amongst the poorest, and were identified as one particular target group to be assisted in escaping absolute poverty. The anti-poverty approach to women is based on the assumption that women's poverty and inequality with men are attributable to their lack of access to productive assets such as land, capital, and to sexual discrimination in the labour market.[2]

At a practical level, this approach to women manifests itself in the proliferation of income-generation projects, in activities which are traditionally done by women, rather than introducing them to new areas of work. Most of these are labour intensive, low paid, low status activities, and in many instances, it is questionable whether they even increase women's income. The focus was on women's productive role with no recognition of their reproductive role and responsibilities.

Undoubtedly, the concept of meeting basic needs through increasing income earning opportunities is a valid one. However, it is the strategy for assisting low income women that must be questioned. Under the anti-poverty approach there was little investment in women themselves, in developing and upgrading their skills either technical or market-related, or giving them access to more profitable skills traditionally dominated by men. For example, women tended to be involved in handicrafts such as basket making and sewing, while men operated in the more profitable areas, for example, as blacksmiths, silversmiths and house builders.

More significantly, the approach focused on how women could be integrated into existing development initiatives rather than questioning why women had fared less well from development strategies in the past decade; neither did it challenge existing patterns of inequality. In this way, the anti-poverty approach accepted the status quo and concentrated narrowly on addressing women's economic poverty with no regard to their social and political poverty. It should be emphasised that even today, a majority of the projects and programmes of donors and non-governmental organisations lie within this women-in-development approach, rather than adopting a gender approach which focuses on women's social relations with men. This reflects an underlying assumption that women will be able to bring about a change in gender relations once they have greater economic independence. It overlooks society's expectation that women perform all tasks and assume responsibility for the care and maintenance of the family, regardless of the amount of time or energy they invest in earning an income. There is no such expectation of men. Women labourers on road construction in Lesotho spent over fifty per cent of their income employing other women in childcare, housework and field work.[3] Many projects introduce appropriate technologies to reduce women's workload so that they can pursue productive activities. While these technologies may benefit individual women (who can afford them), they do little to break down the traditional division of labour.

The approach also ignores the reality that many women are not able to control the income they earn, or that the income is appropriated by men. A forest department in India saw itself as making a significant contribution by employing up to eighty per cent women in its nurseries but closer investigation showed that none of the women were permitted to control the income they earned but had to hand it over to their husbands.

Transfer of Responsibility from the State to Women
Since the mid-1980s, economic recession and debt has caused countries

to adjust their economies, but the measures taken to bring about recovery have had relatively more negative effects on women than men in general, and on specific groups of women, in particular. Just as emphasis is placed on making economies more efficient, the focus on women is to improve their productive contribution within the framework of the market place. In poorer sectors of the population in many developing countries, women have primary responsibility for feeding and caring for their families - that is, for the care and maintenance of the future generation. Consequently, much of the negative impact of cuts or stagnation in government spending in the social sectors such as withdrawal of food subsidies, cuts in health, education and community services, and the introduction of user fees, have had to be absorbed by women. As payment is increasingly required for services formerly provided by the state, women work harder and longer hours to earn the income, and more women are to be found in the informal sector and in prostitution.

Structural adjustment economic policies have served to reinforce the social poverty of women and their children where they lack access to basic services essential for their dignified existence. The negative social effects of adjustment policies compound women's poverty and increase their already heavy work burden. Many are obliged to enter low pay, low status employment or to work in the informal sector, trying to eke out a living. Much time and effort is spent seeking out bargains or working to provide services at the community level - for example, running health clinics. Harsh decisions have to be made; for example, older daughters will be taken out of school to care for young siblings while mothers are out working.[4] Yet, there is real concern regarding the overestimation of 'the ability of women to take up the slack, compensating for low wages and rising prices by new income generating activities'.[5]

Women are very creative and resilient in response to difficult situations. In Calcutta, women explained their survival strategy of shopping at the end of the market day so that they will get bargains, but they are also left with the poorest quality food. In Uganda, a beautiful country struggling with the very high incidence of HIV/AIDS infection, the government has but limited resources to assist its people. Here, as in many parts of Africa, women have taken on a more visible role and are assuming responsibility for the care of the terminally ill and are having a say in community affairs. These examples highlight the ingenuity of women in trying to ensure the survival of their families; however, women are not being allowed to contribute to the development of the wider community nor to the political process, because of poverty of power.

Gender and Development: Understanding Gender

In the mid-1980s questions began to be asked, especially by women from developing countries, regarding the benefits to women of the economic growth and development that was being pursued by

110

governments, and for which they were adjusting their economies often at the behest of international financial institutions.[6] Donors were in the mould of 'mainstreaming women in development', i.e. integrating women into the existing development structures and processes. Indeed, a decade later, with roughly 1 billion of the world's population of 5.3 billion living below the physical poverty line, of which seventy per cent are women, the question whether women want to be integrated into existing structures is a pertinent one. It is out of this context that the gender and development approach emerged.

The gender and development (GAD) approach looks at all aspects of women's lives, and adopts a holistic perspective by examining social, economic and political factors that underlie gender relations. Unlike the WID approach that focused on women as the problem and from which the solution must be found, GAD is concerned with the social relations between men and women; it questions the validity of roles that have been ascribed to men and women by society, and calls for a re-examination of social structures and institutions. It also investigates 'the ways in which [men] assert their masculinity or dominance, and how even the most economically and socially disadvantaged amongst them exert power over women'.[7]

A gender approach tries to understand how relationships between women and men influence development. Central to the relations between women and men are the different roles they play. These are determined by the society in which they live, and are influenced by culture, race, ethnicity, class and location, unlike sex roles which have their basis in the biological differences between men and women. When we talk about gender, therefore, we are not talking about men or women, but the social relationship between them. Gender is a fundamental variable for analysis of social life just like class, race or ethnicity, and it is the basis for a division of labour.

In every society men and women play different roles and perform different functions at work, in the home and in the community, and have different needs relating to these roles. Practical gender needs relate to women's day-to-day needs for family survival and usually relate to unsatisfactory living conditions and lack of resources, while strategic needs arise out of their subordinate position to men.[8] In virtually all societies women not only biologically reproduce children, but society ascribes to them the social role of the carers of the family, the children, the sick and elderly. Women are primarily responsible (unlike men) for family welfare and health, for preparation (and often provision) of food, cooking, washing, cleaning and sanitation, and in rural communities, for the collection of water and firewood. Their reproductive responsibilities encompass these activities, and place demands on their time, energy and resources seven days a week, regardless of other functions they perform in the workplace or in the community.

In common with men, women are also engaged in productive activities such as food production, making handicrafts, involvement in numerous types of small scale trading, and selling their labour as maids, farm labourers, factory workers or piece rate workers based at home. As economies become more cash oriented, and government investment in provision of basic services reduces or stagnates, women are forced to engage in almost any type of economic activity that will earn cash so that they can pay for food, school fees, and health services. Yet, women's unemployment and underemployment usually goes unrecorded in national statistics, and generally, a greater value is put on men's work. In Lesotho, where up to eighty per cent of labourers are women, they form the backbone of road construction under the civil works food-for-work programme. When roads are constructed with payment in cash, men form eighty per cent of labourers.

In many societies, women also play a community service role in that they support, on a voluntary basis, the organisation, management and running of community services, yet they are rarely involved in decision-making that affects the community. Decisions are taken by men, for example settlement of disputes, allocation of land, determining priorities for government assistance, running health services. For example, young educated women from the slums of Calcutta are trained as community health workers, are integral to the state's health care service, and carry out outreach health education on a daily basis. However, they are not state employees, are only paid a stipend as their work is seen to be voluntary, they are not entitled to maternity or annual leave, yet they advise on maternal health.

The lack of understanding of the different gender roles and responsibilities of men and women, and the assumption that the perspective of men and women is the same, is largely to blame for the virtual exclusion of women and their needs from development initiatives over the two decades.

Protection by Father, Husband, Son

A poverty of power dominates women's lives and permeates virtually all aspects of their existence. In most situations women are subjected to the power and decisions of men, whether it be father, husband or son at the household level, or village leaders and politicians at the village and state levels respectively. A key focus of the GAD approach is on strengthening women's legal rights. In many countries, whether in countries that have socialist principles or those that have embraced free enterprise, the civil law of states serves to reinforce the discriminatory nature of customary law, both of which act as barriers to the empowerment of women. In numerous countries, the gender implications of law results in women being considered as minors, firstly they are subject to their fathers, then to their husbands, and lastly to their sons. A husband gains control over his wife and her property in Swaziland and Lesotho, while widows lack property rights on the death of their husbands in Sierra Leone, Tanzania, Uganda and Kenya. A daughter can use, but not own, her father's land in Kenya. The Basotho government signed the Convention on the Elimination of all Forms of

Discrimination against Women on the eve of the FWCW with the exception of those articles that relate to rights under marriage. This opting out means that married women continue to be deprived of inheritance rights. Twenty two countries in sub-Saharan Africa have signed the Convention, but their constitutions do not bar sex discrimination.[9]

In Togo, courts have upheld discriminatory customs which deny women equal rights in property, despite the constitution which outlaws sex discrimination; regarding inheritance, in Togo women are dispossessed when their husbands die, and a daughter cannot receive a share of the cash that may have been derived from the sale of her father's property. A widow's property rights may terminate on remarriage in Kenya (a man's would not); on divorce, a widow may not get financial support for children in Namibia. In Botswana, a woman cannot pass on citizenship to her children.[10]

Gender differences also permeate the economic sector; in the Ivory Coast a husband has the legal right to oppose his wife's business but she cannot oppose his. Most credit laws and practices require collateral in the form of land or other productive assets which is generally inaccessible to women for example Ghana and Kenya. In Lesotho a woman cannot gain credit in her own right nor enter into a contract (for example of employment) without her husband's permission. Zoning and licensing laws which restrict commercial activities to certain areas are likely to limit the access of women to urban markets because they have less freedom of movement than men. Travel to neighbouring countries for raw materials and markets are restricted for women in Swaziland as government practice requires the written permission of a male relative before issuing a passport to a woman. Protective labour legislation excludes women from the most lucrative jobs for example mine work, and often times, night work. In Swaziland, the basic right to health is dependent on men - customary law requires that a woman must provide written consent from her husband or male relative to receive medical treatment from a hospital or clinic.

Evidence is emerging that women are resisting their menfolk where it is not in their own interests to conform. For example, women in outgrower tea farming in Kenya 'sometimes withdraw their labour as a source of leverage to induce their partners to meet their responsibilities towards their families. The household is a site of control, but also of struggle'.[11]

Changing laws does not necessarily affect cultural and traditional practices with regard to women, but when national legislation condones the negative aspects of customary law, equality of rights cannot exist. It is for this reason that the FWCW placed such emphasis on ending all forms of discrimination against women under legislation.

Policy and Practice: Husbands and Donors

There is grave concern today that the gender issue is being accorded lip-service by the development community, many of whom have adopted the relevant terminology and incorporated it into their documents, but do little else. This is because in essence, the GAD approach challenges the status quo - social institutions and structures at the national, household and intra household levels. The WID approach, which dominates in projects and programmes is considered safe and tends to focus primarily on meeting women's practical, immediate needs. Many of the gains that were made under the WID approach in the 1970s were lost in the 1980s because of the impact of structural adjustment economic policies. Adopting a WID or GAD approach is not necessarily an indicator of an agency's commitment to gender issues unless it is supported by resources - personnel, finance, training. The FWCW has given a new impetus to further the gender debate, but the problem that remains is how to translate gender analysis and gender-aware policies into practice.

Development models have tended to reinforce women's powerlessness by failing to take account of the inequalities between men and women. At the household level, it has been assumed that the development of one group of people will automatically benefit others (trickle across), or that if assistance is given to the head of household (seen as the man), all within the family will benefit equally. Experience has shown that this is rarely the case. Depending on their starting point, people respond to and benefit from development activities differently, and this is certainly the case for men and women.

At a policy and implementation level, the main focus has been on mainstreaming women in development into existing development strategies and priorities. However, there is a growing realisation, especially among women from the South, of the need to distinguish between integrating women into existing mainstream development, and the need for transforming the development agenda with a gender perspective. The integrationist approach takes each issue and adapts it to reflect women and gender concerns; for example, detailing gender issues in different sectors. The agenda setting strategy considers women's participation as decision-makers as central in determining development priorities, objectives and goals. There is an inherent tension for women, between the need to try to enter mainstream institutions, agencies and projects in order to transform them, and a concern that working within the system may cause development agencies to lose sight of this goal.

Changing the development agenda is not only about enabling women to participate in development activities, or consulting with women. These are prerequisites in the fight against poverty and inequality. Neither is it sufficient to have projects specifically for women such as those which accompanied the anti-poverty approach, discussed earlier, or welfare projects which primarily see women in their motherhood role. Changing the development agenda is a gradual process for which there are no easy solutions. However, it requires the adoption of an approach which acknowledges women's roles and the related power they have in fulfilling these roles and responsibilities, and giving those who know most about poverty in all its manifestations and its impact - those who endure poverty - control over their own lives, physically, economically, politically and socially. This should be the essence of development policy.

Listening to Women

While there is a recognition in most Southern countries of the need for greater gender equity, there is a deep concern that the policies, strategies and instruments for change are being determined by the donors, and that their Southern partners are required to respond to these rather than setting the agenda themselves. Women need space and resources to enable them to establish their own priorities and to determine how they wish to pursue these priorities. Central to the GAD approach is organisation, which affords an opportunity for women to share views, and analyse their situation and its underlying causes. Development agencies should support them in doing so in order that women can broaden their choices and opportunities. If a positive impact is to be made on alleviating poverty then women's existing power, resilience, roles and work must be recognised and enhanced, while the constraints they face must be addressed. This must take place within an overall approach to development which empowers women and men generally. If women are engaged in the process of decision-making and implementation, they themselves will guide and lead development efforts in the way that is most beneficial for them.

The clarity with which women understand the constraints which face them was exemplified by a woman in the slums of Calcutta, who had been sewing nightdresses for fourteen years at twelve pence per dozen nightdresses. She said she didn't know how to make other types of clothes and could not diversify her products. When asked whether she would attend skills training if it were available, she answered 'yes, if you bring the training near to me'. With this simple direct answer, the woman identified her gender-specific constraints, and a solution to these. She was communicating that she did not have skills to diversify her products and therefore, increase her income; because of her family responsibilities and the fact that her husband doesn't allow her to travel far from the home, she has no option, but to stay in enslaved labour to the same middleman for fourteen years. She also provided the solution - 'give me access to skills training near my home, and I will use the opportunity. Provide training at a central location and I will not be able to attend'. This example shows that it is imperative to recognise women's knowledge and experience, not only concerning their problems, but also on the nature of development interventions.

Isolating Women

At a project level, the lack of participatory processes in general, and specifically to engage women's participation, has resulted in men's lives, perspectives, priorities and needs being adopted as the norm, by governments, donors and extension workers. Where WID/GAD issues are considered, there continues to be much debate on how to operationalise and implement these approaches. Three strategies have been adopted at the project level to address WID: separate projects for women which are usually limited in scope and are labour intensive, adding on a women's component to larger projects, and integrated projects that have a gender-aware approach from the design stage. There is no definitive right and wrong strategy; some situations may require that special provisions be made for women, in mainstream projects, while others present certain gender constraints which can only be overcome through women-specific projects. Most donors favour an integrationist strategy which targets both women and men in all development interventions.

The evidence suggests that the majority of development assistance still fails to reach women and there is a call for a more holistic gender approach rather than a WID approach. To achieve this, projects must focus their analysis on those on whom poverty presses mostly - women. There is need to look at women's lives in their totality and to identify with women the range of needs and constraints they face, and their priorities and preferences, compared with those of men. This can be done through conducting a gender analysis at the project identification stage. Participatory processes, for example, participatory rural appraisal (PRA), which involve a range of men and women (separately if necessary), should be used. The analysis should include examining the division of labour, access to and control of resources, likely distribution of project benefits within the community and within households, an indication of change over time and the factors that have influenced such change. Project appraisal should assess the potential for participation of women as contributors, beneficiaries and agents of change, and assess whether the project will reinforce or has the potential to influence traditional roles and division of labour.

Conclusion

Despite their value to individuals, development projects are limited in terms of their transformational capacity, and many reinforce rather than redress women's subordinate position. The process of change must come from men and women, within societies and communities themselves, supported by the state and other development players. 'Few who have studied women's position would conclude that fundamental change for women ... can be based solely on increasing their individual earning power. Feminist theorists have identified collective action as a primary step for women in achieving personal power and status in the public domain.'[12]

Through organisation, women can share experiences, develop confidence, skills and a sense of self-pride regarding their work, role in the family and society. Women's organisations vary in terms of their objectives and perspectives,[13] but an important distinction is between the extent to which they have a transformative perspective that includes the empowerment of women, and the extent to which they focus on enabling women to cope with the status quo.[14] The experience of women's organisations in the South is that these two goals are complementary rather than mutually exclusive, as women's practical needs must be met before tackling their strategic needs.[15]

As substantial funds are now channelled towards northern and southern NGOs, (which now handle thirteen per cent of official aid), the challenge to donors is to support the organisation of women at a local and national level as an objective in itself. There must be concern that the trend by donors primarily to fund projects that are often geared towards service provision and poverty alleviation, (services that the state should probably provide, in any event), places women in the unenviable position of having to absorb the negative impacts of structural adjustment policies, and deflects their energies away from the underlying causes of their economic, social and political poverty.

Development policies and programmes should recognise basic human needs as human rights, seek to support both the fulfilment of women's practical gender needs, and organisations and processes where women share in determining priorities and making decisions. Meeting those needs means enabling the poor to identify what they want, and what they don't want; it calls for an understanding of the structure of society and the household, the relations between men and women and how these influence development; it requires both men and women to mobilise and work together to bring about societal change; it requires governments to enact and enforce equality before the law; it calls for participative, gender-oriented research; and necessitates providing women with the wherewithal to transform their lives socially, politically and economically. The progress made at the Fourth World Conference on Women in Beijing is another milestone in this process.

NOTES:
1. Goutier, H 'The Hundred Flowers of Women's Diplomacy in Beijing' in *The Courier*, Nov-Dec 1995.
2. Buvinic, M 'Projects for Women in the Third World: Explaining their Misbehaviour' in *World Development*, vol 14(5), 1986.
3. Jennings, M Report to Irish Aid on the Labour Construction Unit in Lesotho, December 1995, unpublished.
4. Moser, C 'The Impact of Recession and Structural Adjustment at Micro-level: Low Income Women and their Households in Guayquil, Equador' in *Invisible Adjustment*, vol 2. UNICEF, 1989b.
5. Baylies, C & Bujura, J 'Challenging Gender Inequalities' in *Review of African political Economy*, no 56, ROAPE Publications, 1993, p.6.
6. Sen, G & Grown, C 'Development Crisis and Alternative Visions: Third World Women's Perspectives', DAWN, New Dehli, 1985.
7. Baylies, C & Bujura, J 'Challenging Gender Inequalities' in *Review of African political Economy*, no 56, ROAPE Publications, 1993, p.3.
8. Molyneaux, M 'Mobilisation without Emancipation? Women's Interests, State and Revolution in Nicaragua' in *Feminist Studies*, vol 11(2), in Moser,

C. 'Gender Planning in the Third World: Meeting Practical and
Strategic Needs' in *World Development*, vol 17(11), 1989.

9. Martin, D M & Omar Hashi 'Women in Development: The Legal Issues in
        Sub-Saharan Africa Today' Working Paper No 4, Policy and Social
        Policy Division, The World Bank, June 1992.

10. *ibid.*

11. Baylies, C & Bujura, J 'Challenging Gender Inequalities' in *Review of
        African political Economy*, no 56, ROAPE Publications, 1993, p.6.

12. Bruce, J 'Homes Divided' in World Development, vol 17(17) taken from
        Elson, D (ed) 'Male Bias in Development Process', Manchester
        University Press, 1991, p.191.

13. Sen, G & Grown, C 'Development Crisis and Alternative Visions: Third
        World Women's Perspectives', DAWN, New Dehli, 1985.

14. Elson, D 'Male Bias in Development Process', Manchester University Press,
        1991.

15. Molyneaux, M 'Mobilisation without Emancipation? Women's Interests,
        State and Revolution in Nicaragua' in *Feminist Studies*, vol 11(2), in
        Moser, C 'Gender Planning in the Third World: Meeting Practical and
        Strategic Needs' in *World Development*, vol 17(11), 1989a.

Meeting Women's Needs: The Challenge of Afghanistan

Ann Kiely

Introduction

Afghanistan is a country with a long history of conflict and instability. It is a land-locked country in South-east Asia, bordered by Turkmenistan, Uzbekistan, and Tajikistan (all republics of the former Soviet Union) to the north, Pakistan to the east and south, and Iran to the west. It shares a short border with China in the north-east.

This part of the world has been overrun by invaders and adventurers from earliest times. It was on some of the great trading and exploration routes of the past. It is not surprising, therefore, that there is such diversity among the peoples of Afghanistan. There are about ten different ethnic groups, of which the main ones are the Pashtuns (who call themselves 'Afghan'), the Tajiks, the Uzbeks, and the Hazaras.[1] There are strong religious, cultural, and traditional differences between them.

At one level, the current instability is due to the conflict that has been going on for about fifteen years, since the Soviets invaded. Even though the Soviets have long since withdrawn, the different groups, many of whom were united in resisting the Soviets, are now at loggerheads and, so far, all attempts to resolve the situation have failed. No one group or alliance has overall control, and the situation is continually changing - 'the political scene is characterised by shifting alliances and extreme fluidity'.[2]

The capital of Afghanistan is Kabul, and the 'government', led by Professor Rabbani, is based there. The quotation marks are used as this government is not widely accepted and its sphere of influence has become very small in recent months, though it still manages to hold Kabul. It is bitterly opposed by relative newcomers to the Afghan cocktail, the Talebaan. In the early weeks of 1995, many people thought that Kabul would fall to the Talebaan who were 'sweeping all before them'. Nevertheless, government forces repulsed the Talebaan attack and, at the same time, pushed back all other opposing forces out of firing range of the city. Since then the whole city has been under government control. Between September and early December of 1995, the city was once again under attack - sometimes fierce - but the government has held on and even managed to consolidate its position a little in the early days of December.

Afghanistan was a poor country even before the present situation developed, and most of its people are very poor. The exact population is not known, but is estimated to be in the region of nineteen million. Several million are in exile, most of them refugees. Nevertheless, there is a strong and on-going tradition of trading - even if some of it 'results from opium production and the systematic stripping and export of public assets'.[3] It is quite obvious that all kinds of goods are available in Kabul, for example, and that there are people who can afford to buy expensive consumer goods. An Oxfam report, written in April 1995, remarks on how the Kabul economy seems to be 'remarkably robust' to outside eyes. The writer surmises that this may be due to its history as a trading city and its location on a number of 'important regional trade routes', but goes on to state that 'it is also a reflection of desperation as many people are forced into economic activity to earn some kind of a living'.[4] For all that there may be a number of very wealthy people, it is still the case that most people live in dire poverty.

International aid agencies of all kinds have been working in Afghanistan for years, but not necessarily in Kabul. There are a few agencies that have operated in Kabul for a long time, but most are relative newcomers. In the last few years, many of the agencies based themselves in Peshwar, just across the border in north-west Pakistan. Given the relatively calm conditions of the spring and summer of 1995, it was anticipated that many agencies would relocate to Kabul. This did not happen to any great extent, for reasons that are not entirely clear.

Oxfam has had a 'connection' with Afghanistan since 1989. In 1991, a support office was set up in Kabul, to serve programmes in central Afghanistan. When fighting started in 1992, this office was moved to Mazar I Sharif in the northern province of Balkh. (Oxfam never operated out of Peshwar.) Following the events of the early months of 1995, Oxfam sent a team to assess the situation and to advise on a possible Oxfam intervention in Kabul city, to add to existing programmes in other parts of the country. The team recommended that Oxfam start a programme of assistance in Kabul, but requested that another team would set up an office in Kabul and examine the situation more closely before final decisions on the nature of Oxfam's programme would be made.[5] This was done in the summer and autumn of 1995. Arising out of the work of the second team, Oxfam is now embarking on a programme that has three main components: working with a consortium consisting of a number of international agencies and the water authority on the restoration of the city water supply; a special distribution of plastic sheeting, blankets and warm clothing for the winter; and an environmental health programme, directed at women specifically, that will also look at ways in which poor women might be able to earn an income.

This paper will describe the situation of the people who live in Kabul city and will look at the specific causes and effects of poverty in the city. It goes on to look at the situation of women, in particular, and finishes by discussing the difficulties faced in trying to decide how best to help.

Kabul City

Kabul is situated to the north-east of the country, at a high elevation and is ringed by high mountains. The Kabul river flows through it. Kabul has a continental climate, being hot in summer (but its elevation and dryness make it much more bearable than other parts of the country) and very cold in winter.

Although there are several large cities in Afghanistan, Kabul is by far the most important. It is both the 'most-Afghan' and the 'least-Afghan' of all of them. Even now when the title of 'capital city' is virtually meaningless and Kabul is isolated from the rest of the country, many Afghans still think of it as being the sophisticated and cosmopolitan heart of Afghanistan. It was historically well-known to all kinds of foreign travellers and visitors and was on the 'hippy-trail' to India in the 1960s and 1970s.

A middle class, comprising highly-educated, liberal, and well-travelled men and women, was well established in the city. Kabul was the capital during the time of the Soviet occupation of Afghanistan. Those people who for reasons of religious belief or other factors were strongly anti-Communist left, and many of them joined the Muahadin. Those who remained became government employees, and many of them took up scholarships and training in the Union of Soviet Socialist Republics (USSR) or associated countries.

In contrast to what happened in other parts of the country, Kabul escaped intact until 1992. Since then, it has suffered a series of prolonged and destructive attacks. Parts of the city, especially the heart of 'old' Kabul and other areas to the south, have suffered very severe damage. Each new attack has resulted in a fresh wave of people leaving the city, or moving from one part of the city to another.

It appears that it was the wealthier people who left the city - either to other parts of Afghanistan or to Pakistan or Iran. Some people who remained in the city as a matter of principle, but many of those who stayed were too poor to have an option. Many have been killed or seriously injured and most families have been affected by the frequent rocket attacks. Since October 1995 there has been consistent rocketing - two to three attacks a day - and sporadic bombing.

Effects of the Conflict

The most visible effect of the conflict is the damage and destruction that has been done to many buildings, roads, and services. In those parts of the city that have been worst affected, private houses, business premises, schools, mosques, and clinics have been destroyed indiscriminately. The main water supply scheme is inoperable and hundreds of thousands of people depend on shallow wells for water (inappropriate and potentially unsafe for a densely populated area where sanitation is poor). There is no electricity except for those who are wealthy enough to own and operate generators.

The 1995 population of the city is estimated to be just over one million people (no official figure is available, but the figure of one million is used by most relief agencies). The population is unevenly distributed, with overcrowding in some districts of the city, while other districts are empty.

There has been no overt breakdown of law and order in Kabul, but many people live in fear of being attacked, robbed or kidnapped and held to ransom. Government services are almost non-existent because of the lack of money and, in some cases, the personnel to provide them. Those who are government employees continue to receive a salary, provided that they actually appear at their place of work. The salary they receive is very small and its purchasing power is low. Even so, people on a government salary are immeasurably better off than the large number of people who have no regular job.

Most families have lost at least one relative to rocket attacks. Others have lost men who went to fight on one or other of the many different 'sides'. Hundreds of people have been maimed as a result of rocket attacks or the widespread minefields. One woman whom I knew personally lost her sister in this way: her family had moved from their own home to live with relatives in another, safer part of the city. During a prolonged lull in the fighting, her father, brother, and sister went back to their own house to check it, as looting was very common. They found the house to be quite secure and went out into the garden for a while. Her sister was particularly fond of the garden and walked around tending to the plants. As she stood near one of the rose bushes she was killed by a rocket. Her father and brother saw this happening but were powerless to do anything. She was 23 years old.

During the summer of 1995, when the city was relatively peaceful and the weather kind, some people began to move back into their own houses. Roughly 169,000 people returned to Kabul, mainly from the refugee camps to the east of the city. Many of the houses that were abandoned had been very badly damaged, and they had to be made habitable once more. It is a feature of the city that the market is flourishing and all kinds of materials are available - at a price. To purchase enough material to carry out even the most basic of repairs puts the average family under great strain. The poorer families are in a hopeless situation, though some have received a little help from the aid agencies.

Transportation is a continuing problem for Kabul people. Fuel is both scarce and very expensive. This means that public transport is in short supply and any other form of transport (apart from pushbikes) is too expensive for most people to afford. Getting to and from work every day is very difficult.

Degrees of Poverty

In the spring of 1995, members of some of the international aid agencies working in Kabul attempted to analyse the nature of the poverty in the city. They described a 'circle of poverty' onto which so many poor people became locked:

'A poor family loses home and moves in with family or friends. The breadwinner becomes (usually only one) sick/unable to work or person who is earning loses job any kind of income; everyone eats less and becomes less healthy' (Based on 'Circle of Poverty' developed by the Kabul Emergency Programmes group, Kabul, 1995).

By some definitions, almost all Kabul people could be described as 'poor', but the Kabul Emergency Programmes Group identified degrees of poverty. Four groups were described as being particularly vulnerable: 1. Widows (and their families); 2. Disabled people (and their families); 3. Elderly people living alone; 4. Urban nomads.

1. Widows
Because of the male casualties in the conflict, those women who lost their husbands and were not able to earn an income themselves, and those who had no male relatives who could help, were thought to be in especially poor circumstances.

2. Disabled People
This refers to cases where the 'breadwinner' of a family is disabled and unable to work. The Kabul Emergency Programme group considered that in a situation where any kind of job was at a premium and where educated and trained people were taking jobs as labourers, the chances of a disabled person being able to get any kind of employment were very small.

I met one woman who had lost her husband and who had herself lost the use of her legs in a rocket attack. She was left with five young children. Her elderly parents lived with her also. She got around in a wheelchair and tried to collect some money by begging - all the others were dependent on her.

3. Elderly People
This was a rather vague classification. The number of elderly people without a family is probably not very large, though again the conflict has given rise to situations that would have been almost unheard of in past times.

4. Urban Nomads
I have heard Kabul people who are living in rented accommodation describing themselves as 'homeless', that is, they are not living in their own homes. The urban nomads are a particularly badly-off group of homeless people. They are the people who have lost their own homes, moved in with relatives or friends for a while, but eventually have had to take rented accommodation. Finding it difficult to pay the rent they are then forced to move on to another cheaper place where they manage for a while and then leave once more. With each move they lose more of their possessions, and are all the time growing poorer and poorer. These nomads are unlikely ever to be able to repair or rebuild their original homes.

I was told of one very poor family whose home was destroyed. This family moved to another part of the city, to cramped rented accommodation. The father of the family had poor health and was disabled (not from the fighting) and earned a small income from mending shoes. The children were young. They reached a point where they were no longer able to pay the rent and had to move out. They ended up in a hut in a timber yard, a dark and unhealthy place. Some of the children are pedlars and they bring home a little money. This family missed out on the help from the agencies because 'no one guessed that anyone was living in such a place'.

Women

Prior to the current conflict, many Kabul women had been used to going to work and earning their own living. Many had a high standard of education and some had been given the chance to study abroad. However this is only part of the picture. There is a very high illiteracy level in Afghanistan (sixty-eight per cent in 1992), especially among women - of the thirty-two per cent of Afghans who are literate only thirty-two per cent are female.[6] Prior to the conflict some illiterate women did go out to work, to do jobs like cleaning and tailoring, but most did not. Among the more strictly religious and/or traditional families, women are not allowed out either to work or school.

Restrictions were imposed on women and their movements in the early days after the fall of the Communist-backed regime. They were forbidden to go out to work and a strict dress code was put in place. A former colleague of mine told how, when she heard the announcement that women were to 'cover-up', she made up sets of the most glamorous pantaloons she could design. The legs had to be covered at all times, so pantaloons would be worn under skirts. When women are enveloped in the chaudhur, the legs from the knee down, enclosed in the pantaloons, may be seen. She knew that she had to submit, but was determined to make a small protest.

Over time, these rules were relaxed so that now restrictions are more likely to be imposed by individual families than by regulation of the authorities. The rule forbidding women to go out to work is still 'on the books' and it is difficult for them to obtain the work permits that all employed Afghans are obliged to hold. It appears that the authorities turn a blind eye to this however and women do work, with or without permits. (This is not the case in other parts of the country where the Talebaan are in power.)

For programme purposes, Oxfam carried out an exercise involving an informal examination of the lives of women in those areas of the city worst affected by the conflict. This was done with the help of an Afghan non-governmental organisation called Co-operation for Reconstruction of Afghanistan (CRA). It was a simple exercise in which a number of women who were themselves living in those areas went around to visit other women and engaged them in conversation about their lives and times. Contact was made with more than 800 women during October and November of 1995. Although the information is mainly anecdotal and not subject to any scientific analysis, some patterns were obvious. It was also illuminating to hear the views and opinions of the 16 women who carried out the exercise. These were well-educated, working women from various backgrounds. None of them could be considered very well-off, but compared to many of the women they interviewed, they were fortunate.

The lack of income and the difficulty in securing one came up time after time as being the most pressing factor in the lives of these women and their families. This applied to all kinds of families, including those with able-bodied men. However, it was particularly critical for those widows who did not have adult male relatives or sons.

One of the most interesting features of the exercise, was the light it shed on how almost all of the families were managing to survive. Educated women had an advantage in that many of these would have worked previously and were continuing their jobs (teachers, university lecturers, civil servants, and so on). Women who were illiterate were very limited in the kind of work that they could get. Some of them tried to eke out a living by doing some tailoring or dress-making in their homes. Others did cooking in their homes and their children would sell the food on the streets or in the markets. Many were dependent solely on their young children going out and peddling every day. Some women were making kites for sale out of plastic carrier bags and little bits of wood. The income from any of these activities would be very small. There was an account of a widow with six young children. Her husband had been killed in a rocket attack and she had no male relative to help her. She was illiterate but she did go out to work - as a cleaner in one of the hospitals. She received a small wage for this work and the doctors were kind to her and she was able to bring food home for her children. However, she sometimes had to work at night and then her children were alone. They lived in very poor rented accommodation, and none of the children were going to school.

Another account tells of a thirty-year-old woman, again with young children, whose husband had disappeared two years before. They had been living in a house owned by her father-in-law. All her own relatives had left Kabul and gone to live in the north of Afghanistan. After her husband's disappearance, she decided to go and live with her own parents. The day she arrived at her parent's house, her father died and a short time later her mother died too. She decided after all this to come back to Kabul. On her return she discovered that her father-in-law had given 'her' house to one of his sons. She then had to go into rented accommodation for which her father-in-law pays. Although literate, she did not work outside of the house and her father-in-law helped her with basic living expenses. She was confident that her husband would come back even though she had no news of him.

One family consisted of two women and four children. Both women had been wives of the same man who had been killed in a rocket attack. Both were illiterate. The elder of the two women was ill and bed-ridden.

The other who was the mother of all four children had the responsibility of looking after all of them. She kept the girls at home to help with looking after the elder woman. The boys went out peddling.

Of the three districts of the city that were included in the study, two were areas that had been badly affected by the fighting and many if not most of the buildings had been damaged or destroyed. The third area had not suffered great damage but had many people living in cramped conditions and the people generally had very low incomes. For the people living in the damaged areas, a very major concern was making their dwelling weather-tight for the winter - many of the buildings were without windows and doors. Most women too were worried about how they would get warm clothing for their children. The onset of winter had other implications too in that it would have become much more difficult for those people who earned something from peddling to venture out.

Other issues that came up were kindergartens (in the past these had been provided at places of work, but now the government is unable to fund them), clinics for women (or, in many cases, just a clinic - clinics were destroyed in the fighting and have not been replaced); literacy classes for women; the desirability of special tailoring/dress-making institutes for women only (based on the reasoning that women who are not allowed out to work would be allowed to attend an exclusively female place where she could earn an income). When the interviewing group was asked why women were looking for literacy classes the reason most often given was that women felt they would be better-off if they became literate.

International Assistance

As will have been gathered from previous sections there are both acute and long-term needs in Kabul, and it seems that it is impossible for the government to satisfy those needs. It is clear that many people though in very poor circumstances, are managing to survive by their own efforts. These are side-by-side with others who are on a slide to total destitution, and will not survive without some form of material support.

The best established agency in Kabul is the International Committee of the Red Cross (ICRC). There are a number of international NGOs, all but a handful of which are purely medical. Both the ICRC and the medical NGOs concentrated on emergency medical assistance during the worst of the fighting. They were also to the fore when people started returning to the damaged parts of the city and there were many mine injuries. They were involved in the relief effort in the early part of 1995, and the ICRC continues a relief programme for disabled people and their families.

The most prominent of the non-medical agencies is the United Nations Centre for Human Settlement (known as Habitat), which has a long and esteemed presence in Kabul. Habitat has initiated what are known locally as 'Neighbourhood Action Programmes' in the worst affected areas of the city. These programmes have elements of sanitation and drainage and are carried out in conjunction with the Kabul

Municipality. They involve discussion and planning with the people living in particular areas. Habitat is the lead agency on a proposed scheme to reinstate the city water supply. There are three international non-medical NGOs that work on water supply and sanitation in various parts of the city. Oxfam is involved in the management team of the water supply scheme and is assisting in equipment selection and provision.

Afghan NGOs, with one or two exceptions, are not very active in Kabul - most of the Afghan NGOs are based in Peshawar.

Apart from Habitat and, perhaps, the World Food Programme (WFP), and the United Nations High Commission for Refugees (UNHCR), the humanitarian agencies of the UN are not particularly active in Kabul. Most of them maintain a presence but their head offices are in Islamabad in Pakistan.

Assistance has tended to be very much of the 'emergency response' type, dealing with acute needs for medical services, food, shelter, and basic water and sanitation facilities. Of course women benefited (and continue to do so) from these efforts - indeed women make up a large part of the 'vulnerable groups' identified by the Kabul Emergency Programme Group, and so have been the recipients of a large part of the assistance that was on offer. In addition, the NGO CARE International has started a project with a group of 1,000 very poor widows, where the women are paid in kind (food) for making quilts and items of clothing.

At the time that Oxfam arrived in Kabul in July, 1995, that was the nature of assistance aimed directly at women. Oxfam places a special emphasis on women to ensure their concerns are taken into account in any programme to be undertaken or supported by Oxfam. As was made plain in earlier sections of this paper, many of the women in Kabul are in very poor circumstances. It was also made clear that very many of them are managing to survive by their own efforts. In such cases the value of outside assistance has to be questioned.

It is not easy to decide how best assistance can be provided. The situation is very complex, not least because Kabul is a large capital city, with a considerable population of poor people - not a typical 'theatre of operation' for many NGOs. The needs and requirements are on a very large scale - a scale usually reserved for the bilateral aid regime. However as long as the situation continues to be unresolved and the Kabul 'government' remains unrecognised by other states, there will be no bilateral aid for Kabul. At the same time, the UN development agencies will not be interested in starting long-term development programmes. In such circumstances, it behoves the NGOs to try and respond to some of the needs.

Taking these constraints into account, in early 1996 Oxfam is to embark on an environmental health programme with women in four districts of the city. An important part of this programme will be the organising of projects whereby women will be able to earn a small income by their own activities. (This is not income generation in the usual meaning of the term, as this is difficult to establish successfully in normal circumstances and would be impossible in Kabul given the present conditions.) These projects are likely to be of the 'local production of relief goods' type, where women would make items that would later be made available for distribution. Another element will be meeting women in their own homes or in larger groups for discussion and, where appropriate, action on matters which impinge on their own health and well-being, and that of their families. This will be tied up with the district level works (water supply, refuse collection, and drainage) that make up the Habitat Neighbourhood Action Programme.

This will be a challenging undertaking - not least because it will be difficult to assess the outcome. Nevertheless, it has the potential to make a difference to the lives of many Kabul women.

NOTES:
1. Overseas Development Authority, 1995.
2. *ibid.*
3. *ibid.*
4. Oxfam, 1995.
5. *ibid.*
6. UNDP, 1994.

BIBLIOGRAPHY:
Kapila M et al (1995), Review of British Aid to Afghanistan, London: Overseas Development Authority; Leader N. et al (1995), Kabul Assessment Report, Oxford: Oxfam.

Development Work in South Sudan:
Obstacles and Opportunities

Deirdre Considine

As an Irish woman working in southern Sudan, the experiences of Sudanese women coping with conflict and the structures and biases of an extremely patriarchal society have had a particular, and personal resonance for me. In Sudan, as in Ireland, women have not only directly or indirectly experienced conflict and division in their own country - they have coped with its aftermath on family and community. Women in both countries have also, although arguably to a much lesser degree in Ireland, been systematically excluded from taking control of their lives or of having a say in their own, or their community's future.

Yet such an attitude is paradoxical, for whilst women are judged inferior by themselves and their own culture, they remain, whether in Ireland or Sudan, the often invisible backbone of their society and a major focus for its regeneration and development.

With such parallels in mind, this chapter looks first at the effects of conflict upon women in southern Sudan and the essential role they play in the survival of their families and communities. It then offers a broad discussion on how Oxfam is trying to implement a gendered approach to its relief and development programmes. The chapter illustrates that discussion by looking at the health programme Oxfam is currently running in one of several operational areas in southern Sudan, that of Rumbek County in Eastern Bahr el Ghazal.

Sudan, Africa's largest country, is a land of diversity. Geographically, this diversity is expressed in arid deserts in the north and west, savannah grasslands in the central regions, and woodlands and swamp in the south. Culturally, Sudan's diversity is expressed in a population of some twenty-six million people that is composed of nineteen major ethnic groups speaking some 113 different languages.

As a result of an economic policy largely adopted when the country was under Anglo-Egyptian rule, development has been biased towards the central regions of the country, at the expense of other areas. Such biased development has continued since the country gained Independence in 1956 and may be seen as a primary cause of civil war that first erupted in that same year. Apart from an interim period of peace - 1972 to 1983 - Sudan has suffered civil war between the Islamic government in the north and minority non-Islamic anti-government forces in the south. Fighting has largely been confined to the southern parts of the country, where an estimated twenty-five per cent of Sudan's population - some six million people - live.

The civil war in Sudan is now the longest running conflict in the world. In common with many similar 'modern' wars, civilians in Sudan have been a major target for all sides engaged in the conflict. The war has been, and still is, characterised by the gross violation of human rights by all combatants, and the mass displacement of civilian populations. The war has also contributed either directly or indirectly to the famines which swept parts of the south in the mid-1980s and early 1990s.

Since 1956, the conflict has caused the deaths of at least one million Sudanese, with an estimated 250,000 people having died in the current round of warfare. The incessant warring has exacted a tremendous human and economic toll on the country, especially women, children and the elderly, particularly in the war-ravaged south of the country which remains the focus of the fighting.

The main opposition force in the south is the Sudan People's Liberation Army (SPLA). In 1991 the SPLA broke into two factions - the Sudan People's Liberation Front (SPLF) and the South Sudan Independence Movement (SSIM). Clashes between the north and south and between southern factions have led not only to thousands of deaths but, according to the UN, the internal displacement of an estimated two million people. In addition to the displaced, more than 250,000 Sudanese have fled abroad, living as refugees mainly in the neighbouring countries of Uganda, Ethiopia and Zaire. Ninety per cent of the displaced and refugees are women and children.

The South

In a country where underdevelopment is the norm, the south remains perhaps the most underdeveloped area not only of Sudan, but, arguably, of Africa as a whole. Years of neglect have resulted in an almost complete lack of investment and basic infrastructure - roads, schools, hospitals, local government and industry.

Since 1983, the infrastructure which existed in the south has been largely destroyed by war and inter-factional conflict between various ethnic groups.

The Gender Dimensions of Conflict

'I get up before the sun comes up and my first girl and I carry our pot and our leaky [plastic] container to the well. There are two other families living near by, both of them, like me, without a husband, and we all go to the well together. My husband is away with another wife and his elder brother was supposed to look after me, but he didn't of course, just left me pregnant and then disappeared! The baby died. I don't know why, she just stopped breathing in the night. We have nothing really, a little sorghum, but not much. I tried to cultivate the land but I was pregnant and it was difficult. There are wild fruits and things, but they are scarce as everyone is trying to live off them. I've been here a good few months now ever since the [Nuer] raid on Akot. We [the women living together] are not related but have just set up here in these old huts.'[1]

In spite of the enormous advances that women have made in the past twenty years to alter the social, cultural and economic discrimination they suffer, and the erroneous and unfounded beliefs concerning women's 'natural' inferiority that they are based upon, such convictions still dominate, by degree, the cultural and socio-economic norms of many, if not all, societies. Globally, men retain more power in both the public and private spheres of their society than women, and, as a result, many women perceive themselves, and are perceived, as subordinate members within a culture of patriarchal dominance.

A woman's role in southern Sudan is seen - by both the women themselves and the society they live in - to lie almost exclusively within this sphere of the household. The maintenance of the family and the well-being of the household are thus the major source of a woman's personal identity and of her status within her society. In times of conflict, displacement, and social and economic marginalisation, this role in the survival of their families and communities becomes even more critical than in times of peace.

Yet in such circumstances, when there is a dramatic reduction in the degree of support available to women to cope with maintaining their children, the sick, the disabled and the elderly, women themselves often suffer a decrease in their social status and esteem. Though the fulfilment of the emotional and economic needs of the family is now often the sole responsibility of women, their position is weakened further. The inequality women and girls experience, and live with daily, becomes sharply magnified in conflict situations. There are several reasons for this.

The Sole Provider

Because husbands, sons or brothers are often absent from their homes in times of conflict, women find themselves head of the family and the often sole providers for themselves, their children and dependants. The UN has estimated that some fifty per cent of southern Sudanese women are, or have been, left in such a situation. This figure rises sharply in displaced or refugee populations where an estimated ninety-five per cent are women and young children. In such circumstances, women find their economic roles greatly extended, now taking on the various productive activities such as building houses, clearing fields and tending livestock which would normally have been done by men.

Traditionally, in Sudanese culture (as indeed in the cultures of most societies in the world), women do most of the so-called 'invisible' reproductive work in the household. They grow the subsistence crops, do the cooking and cleaning, look after the children and older relatives and supply the household utilities such as fuel and water. Research has shown that the average woman's day starts before dawn and ends well after sunset. A routine day for a woman in southern Sudan may involve fetching of water from the traditional well. Trips of up to five kilometres are not unusual to reach the nearest well. The grinding of staple food, sorghum, can take two hours when done by hand. It is a strenuous, time-consuming, onerous task. However, in a conflict area such as southern Sudan, the role of the woman is expanded as they are left behind to maintain the household while the men go to fight the war. Their roles now include all the activities they previously held but they must now also adopt the roles traditionally held by men. Thus, if the family is moved due to the insecurity of an area, it is the women's responsibility to locate an alternative site, and build accommodation for her family. Given the expanded role of the female in such a situation, it falls to a girl child to develop faster than her male sibling as she is expected to assume some of the roles held by her mother. It is said in Sudan that a girl child does not exist, she is born a woman with the responsibilities of a woman from a very young age.

The continuance of cultural values also becomes women's sole responsibility, with women being expected to teach their children customs and the gendered roles expected of them.

However this extension of productive activities and social responsibilities is not accompanied by an increase in women's status within their community. The responsibilities that men are culturally required to undertake towards women, especially widows, through kinship obligations, disappear, as do the mechanisms such as traditional courts of law which upheld such obligations. As communities collapse and fragment so does the status of women within them, leaving them more vulnerable to rape, violence and abuse.

The Health of Women

Health care is a critical area of concern for women and girl children in southern Sudan. There are several areas to health care which have been made more difficult for the woman as the war rages on. A woman is expected to produce as many children as possible during her reproductive years and the inability of a household to be able to provide adequate resources for supporting large families is not considered. A large family is also considered a form of compensation for a husband who has paid the brideprice for his wife. In the event of a husband dying, the woman continues to bear children through the agency of one of her husband's brothers (or even one of his elder sons in the case of a young wife in a large polygamous household).

High infant mortality rates, deaths from war, disease, hunger and displacement and the social customs within the society all pressurise women into having high numbers of pregnancies during their reproductive lives. Women thus become pregnant not only by their absent husband's brother or by another male relative, but increasingly by a man from outside the kinship group. In many cases the women are then abandoned and left with another mouth to feed on their own.

As social pressures to have more children increase, so the practice of spacing births has eroded, with the exception of a few cases where the family kinship unit has remained intact. Repeated pregnancies and early weaning adversely affect the health of the mother and her child, respectively leaving both further malnourished and more susceptible to disease. What has also increasingly broken down is the custom of older women teaching basic ante-natal health care and the customs which surround sexual relationships, to younger women. Rates of pregnancy amongst unmarried girls have thus increased, resulting in many girls and women finding themselves further socially ostracised because of their sexual relations outside of marriage, or standing accused of adultery.

Although the infant mortality rate is not documented in southern Sudan, the majority of women consulted at the Oxfam mother and child health care clinics in Rumbek county have suffered at least one infant death and can recount stories of other mortalities experienced by their female neighbours.

From a combination of overwork, scarcity of food, unclean drinking water, the increased pressure to become pregnant, and the mental and physical insecurity experienced on a daily basis - including the very real likelihood of being raped - women do indeed, to borrow an old African adage, 'hold the sharp end of the knife' in their society.

Lack of Education
Within southern Sudan there is a tradition to send boy children to school in preference to the girl children. There are many factors behind this tradition including greater involvement in the domestic chores of the household from an early age as detailed earlier. Early marriage for Sudanese women (girls can be married as young as thirteen years of age) is another factor for withholding education from the girl child. The southern Sudanese attach a bridewealth to their girl children. The exchange of bridewealth from her prospective husband's family to her parent's family is considered as a fair exchange for their labour and her reproductive capacity. The earlier a girl child is married, the earlier this wealth is realised for her family. Lack of resources within a household to send several children to school also means that priority is given to the boy child. Fear that an education will develop the girl child and render her more difficult to control works against her. Lack of clothing and an inappropriateness for the girl child to attend school naked is cited by elders as another reason for the girl child not to attend school. Thus, even in peaceful times the obstacles for a girl child to achieve an education are monumental. Living in an insecure environment with a lack of teachers due to conflict further undermines the likelihood of the girl child receiving an education.

Because of situations such as these and the pivotal role that women play at such times, humanitarian aid and projects to help rebuild the capacities of societies to cope with war, drought, and displacement, have increasingly focused directly upon women.

Programme Work in SPLA held areas of southern Sudan

Since the 1980s, Oxfam has worked in southern Sudan. Since 1989 it has worked there under the umbrella of the UNICEF and World Food Programme-led Operation Lifeline Sudan (OLS) together with some forty other international and Sudanese non-government organisations (NGOs). OLS operates in both the government and non-government held areas of Sudan to help alleviate the effects of civil war, drought and famine on civilian populations.

The southern Sudanese are reliant upon the INGO/OLS network to bring in everything to the south such as incentives of soap and salt, paid as salary to local workers; demuria for mosquito nets; clothes (apart from those which local southern traders manage to carry by bicycle from the border); primary health care kits from UNICEF; veterinary drugs from OLS and the INGOs; seeds, tools, and fishing equipment. The traders of all such commodities, who were in the main from the north, have long ago ceased from travelling down with these goods to the towns of the south.

Rumbek County, Eastern Bahr el Ghazal, is a remote place, largely accessible only by aeroplane. It is also very insecure, suffering raids between Dinka and Nuer, as well as government and rebel fighting, which affect the viability and continuance of Oxfam's programme work. There are few roads, the best of them no more than the broad straight tracks which are all that remain of a network which, before the war, linked the villages and towns together. All are virtually impassable during the wet season - July to November - and some are also mined. Because of the impassability of the roads during the rains, some of the clinics, such as the one at Agangrial, are dry-season only operations.

Adopting a Gendered Approach to Relief and Development Interventions

Adopting a gendered approach to any relief and development intervention, although it may consist of specific interventions aimed exclusively at women, has to build such interventions from an understanding of the ways in which people relate to one another within a wider framework; a network of interests that intersect in many different ways.

Too often in the past, the term 'gender relations' has been wrongly perceived by many practitioners, particularly, but not solely, by men involved in technical programmes, as exclusively applying to the rights and needs of women, as if such rights and needs were somehow peripheral and of no value and importance to the well-being of society as a whole. Adopting such a viewpoint can, and often does, further marginalise women and so re-enforces the very cultural perceptions that are the root cause of women's inferior position.

Societies are not fixed entities; rather, they are dynamic - a complex system of relationships that change and can be changed in a fluid, open-ended process through space and time. Oxfam's intervention in Rumbek County, Bahr el Ghazal, would obviously lead to some degree of change within such existing relationships, particularly as its work is built upon participation: helping people realise technical and social change largely through their own community-based structures. The central reason for adopting such a participatory approach is the belief that it is the most effective way for people to acquire a greater degree of control over their own development, particularly people who are socially and economically marginalised.

The Challenges of Gender Aware Stategies

A project that is built upon such analysis is, however, faced with many complex problems. How, for example, are existing structures affected by - or resistant to - social and economic change, particularly when a society is itself in a prolonged process of fundamental change and fragmentation through conflict, displacement and insecurity? Similarly, how do such relations affect the project's goals of maximising the participation and empowerment of the whole community? What factors might inhibit participation? What factors promote it?

Oxfam's health programme has concentrated on the rehabilitation of primary health care west of the Nam river, but is now attempting to widen its sphere of activity. Although the work concentrates on all aspects of health care, the overall approach is one of integrating hospitals and clinics into a system that tackles not only the effects of disease but its causes as well. For instance, in tackling water-borne diseases the whole cycle is then dealt with: hygiene at the wells, basic health education such as washing hands - though even soap is hard to get here - and then backing this up with other preventative measures. If this holistic approach is not adopted health care remains stuck in a cycle of treating the symptoms of disease.

Traditional healing, viewed as an art which is passed down from generation to generation in certain families has largely disappeared in this and other areas of the south, and has therefore become another casualty of the war. A few healers, though, continue to practise their craft.

Men remove TB-infected bones, mend broken legs, and clean wounds, whilst women have always played a significant role in other areas of traditional healing. Epilepsy and pneumonia, for example, were treated by women with roots cooked in ground nut oil, and there are other herbal remedies for sterility, rheumatism and mental disorders which, so it is claimed, particularly affect men! The role of traditional birth attendants, a craft handed down through the generations, is also one which has largely ceased to be practised. In such a vacuum, many women have died through want of even the most basic of skilled attention.

As we noted earlier in this chapter, not only has much of the practice of traditional healing been lost, but much of the counselling and knowledge that women passed on to their daughters on sexual behaviour, menstruation, pre-natal and post-natal care has also largely disappeared.

'There are children growing up who know nothing, not even the seasons of the year and what should happen then. As to health, it is as if we have slipped backwards. We have lost all that we knew.'[2]

To northern eyes, much of the work of traditional healers may seem to be based less on sound medical science than on superstition. While this may be so in some cases, what should not be forgotten is the crucial role such practices also play in maintaining a coherent social structure, especially that of the role women play in its maintenance. This is particularly so regarding the wealth of knowledge and experience certain women have about pregnancy and childbirth. The loss of such knowledge further undermines the self esteem and social integrity of a people.

The replacement of traditional health practices and knowledge by a purely western approach can also aid and abet this process. The use of western medicines, particularly drugs, can easily lead to a situation where people see further proof of their own inadequacies and become the passive recipients of drug handouts.

To help prevent such a situation occurring, traditional healers and birth attendants are viewed as an integral part of Oxfam's health programme and integrated into the programme's work. The healers work with local people trained in modern medical techniques and also receive training in these methods themselves. This mix of modern and traditional medicine both helps to introduce the clinic to people and provides traditional healers and birth attendants with the support they need to continue their work.

Involving the Whole Community

The relations which Oxfam has with the local community and with the Sudan Relief and Rehabilitation Agency (SRRA) - the relief wing of the SPLA, which has de facto control of the area - is one which requires patience, understanding and tact. In common with many such situations there is a potential conflict of perceived interests from all sides regarding health care, as in other areas of relief and development work. In an area where there are few, if any, clinics, there can exist fierce competition as to where a clinic is to be placed, for example, and who is to benefit from it.

Similarly, many local people perceive western medicine purely in terms of it being a matter of resources; of supplying curative drugs to people. It is necessary that local decision-makers see the need for a preventative approach to health care based upon community structures. Without involving local people in health care, particularly in teaching basic hygiene and the causes and prevention of certain diseases, any such programme cannot be sustainable.

The other NGO alternative and one which might well be forced upon Oxfam and other NGOs involved in health care programmes if the conflict escalates further, is simply to run vaccination programmes. While such programmes are a vital component of any health programme, they fall far short of what is necessary: a network of clinics that are an integral part of local communities which provide people with the structure, the knowledge and the resources to help prevent and cure diseases.

Involving women in such structures is probably the hardest part of the programme's work. In common with many similar programmes, Oxfam has found that women benefit least from the clinics and the resources they provide.

'The majority of the patients that turn up here each day are men. Women and children are often notable by their absence. Sure, a few do turn up, particularly those women who are pregnant, but by and large, it's men who benefit from the programme.'[3]

Similarly, it is men who exclusively come forward for training as Community Health Workers (CHWs). A major factor in the lack of female CHWs is due to the fact that there is high female illiteracy in the region. Without basic literacy skills, women cannot take notes or read labels on drugs and medicines. A crucial factor in getting women involved is increasing their opportunities for obtaining basic education. As has been noted, educational opportunities are gendered and remain almost exclusively the right of men and boys.

A related problem concerns time and distance. The workload faced by women is, as we have already described above, daunting. They have water to fetch, homes to keep, sorghum to grind, meals to cook, firewood to chop and carry, children and other dependants to keep, as well as fields to cultivate. Thus, they have little time to get involved. The distance women might have to cover to attend a clinic, and the time needed to make such a journey, which might take several hours, also prohibits them from either becoming directly involved in the clinic or utilising it fully. Thus, to attend a clinic would generally only be considered by those who lived close to it, or by those further afield only in a dire emergency.

Female illiteracy and considerations of time and distance are symptomatic of something more fundamental: women's secondary status within their own society. For local men, not only was there more time to get involved, but the clinics also tended to revolve almost exclusively around their own perceptions of what is important and what is not, and, by and large, women's health is largely of secondary concern to them. As an Oxfam health worker explains: 'the clinic is perceived by men as giving them prestige within their own community. Working as a CHW also gives them benefits, especially when they attend training sessions where they can get meals. Of the thirty five traditional birth attendants (TBAs), all of them are women, but I'm sure that, given the chance, men would try and take over this area as well.'

Oxfam has recently begun to explore new ways of involving women as well as men more fully into its programme work. A series of community hygiene awareness programmes has been started which involves a female Oxfam health worker visiting households and talking to women. Such a move has, slowly, begun to address considerations of time and distance and, because it utilises a female health worker who deals directly with other women in their homes, more women have begun to understand that they too have a voice in health matters, particularly those which relate specifically to them. The plan is now to integrate the hygiene awareness programmes into broader village development councils (VDCs) in which women will have a specific role to play, and to link this enterprise into another Oxfam programme that is concerned with digging wells and their maintenance.

What is needed for such initiatives to work, particularly from the perspective of women, is to employ nurses and health workers who are either Dinka or have a working knowledge of the language and Dinka culture. Female health workers are often from other African countries such as Kenya, and almost solely rely on male interpreters when they talk to local women.

'What we found out is that male interpreters were not translating literally what Dinka women were saying, but rather giving us what they, as men, thought that we should know. It was biased from a gendered perspective and kept from us a lot of information that was vital.'[4]

Experiences in livelihood monitoring have run into similar difficulties and the aim is to improve information gathering techniques in this area as well and, eventually, integrate all areas of programme work - health, water, veterinary, food monitoring and food security - into one holistic and dynamic framework. But, as has been outlined above, the difficulties in achieving a fully integrated and fully participatory programme which involves women as well as men are immense, and should be gauged in terms of years rather than months.

A Window of Opportunity?

The loss or the change of their role and status, and the physical and mental suffering experienced by women in times of crisis, often not only force them to adopt new strategies to survive, but many also lead some of them to ask fundamental questions about the society they live in. In Rumbek county, such questioning of their society and their subordinate status within it is slowly taking place.

The prejudices operating against the women demand advocacy both for attitudinal change and economic development. The primary consideration, if sustainable advances are to be made in addressing gendered inequalities, is that they cannot be forced upon a society but rather that society as a whole recognises the need for such changes, and understands the benefits they will bring to the whole community.

However, in other countries that have suffered years of war, famine and displacement but are now attempting to rebuild the shattered structures and fabric of their communities, evidence suggests that gender relations do not significantly change in their fundamental bias towards women, but are simply rearranged.

The conflict may, it is true, have loosened some of the cultural, structural and economic bonds that hold women and thereby have given them an increasing degree of economic and social independence, however such new independence is too often effectively used in justifying the extension of a woman's 'legitimate' work load and what is expected of her, without altering her inferior status.

Thus the empowerment of women remains a long and uphill struggle. If peace does not eventually come to Sudan, it is almost certain that there will be immense problems in maintaining the small and often fragile advances made by women in gaining further control over their lives, and of participating more fully in the economic, social and political life of their communities.

As in Ireland, however, where there have been great advances made by women in attaining greater equality and a greater degree of control over their reproductive rights as well as those relating to their social, economic and political rights, the only sustainable advances are made when society as a whole, no matter how grudgingly or reluctantly, begins to see the simple truth and logic that such movements are based upon. In Sudan, one feels that such a situation may be a long, long way away, but, one day, it will be realised.

NOTES:
1. Akoi Cadai, Akot, Eastern Bahr el Ghazal.
2. Sudanese Oxfam worker, Akot.
3. Oxfam nurse.
4. Kenyan Health Worker.

With Vietnam's move from a centrally controlled to a market economy well under way, the country is set to become another 'Asian tiger'. There are, however, a number of people, including women, disabled, and ethnic minorities who are having difficulties seizing the new opportunities. Hoang Thi Quy is an example: she has three children and an elderly mother. Her husband has left her, and she has no land. Making hats she earns sixty pence for five days work, a third of which goes on materials, and the remaining buys three kilos of rice.
(Going Global: Women and Economic Globalisation by Helen O'Connell)

Photograph by Sean Sprague.

Notes on Contributors

Ann Kiely is a civil engineer who works in the field of emergency relief. She has returned recently from Afghanistan.

Mary Jennings studied social policy and planning for developing countries at the London School of Economics. She now works as a social development consultant, trainer and lecturer, and has extensive experience in applying a gender analysis at the policy and project level across a range of sectors from transport to health, in both Asia and Africa.

Breeda Hickey worked as Emergencies Programme Co-ordinator for Oxfam UK/Ireland in Zaire, Burundi and Rwanda from 1993-1995. She has also worked in Somalia and Sudan, in both emergency and rehabilitation work.

Deirdre Considine is currently working in Nairobi with Oxfam southern Sudan programme. Prior to that she spent two years working in Cambodia, with Concern. Deirdre is a graduate of University College Dublin.

Trish Hegarty is currently working as a regional journalist with the BBC in Derry. Between 1989 and 1995 she worked in Dublin as a freelance journalist, writing largely for *The Irish Times*.

Helen O'Connell is a writer and lobbyist on women's rights, gender and development, and European aid issues. She works as a policy and education coordinator with One World Action, a non-governmental organization based in London. She is also president of Women in Development Europe (WIDE).

Maggie O'Kane is based in London with *The Guardian*. Since she left RTE in 1989 she has covered most of the world's major conflicts, from the fall of the Berlin Wall to the peace in Bosnia, where her writing earned her awards from Amnesty International as well as Britain's highest journalistic awards. She lives in London, with her husband, John Mullin, who is also a *Guardian* journalist.

Penny Cabot is chairperson for Banúlacht - Irish Women for Development.

Róisín Boyd worked in London on *Spare Rib* feminist magazine in the 1980s. She is now a producer and reporter with RTE. She has travelled extensively in Asia, Africa and Central America for the *Worlds Apart* radio series - including Rwanda, Cambodia, Vietnam and the Philippines.

Aileen O'Meara is a radio producer and reporter with RTE Radio 1, working with the *Pat Kenny Show* and *Today at Five*. Formerly a print journalist with *The Sunday Tribune* and the *Irish Press*, she works in the area of current affairs and has travelled widely for RTE, including in Bosnia and Croatia.

Siobhán Creaton, a native of Ballaghaderreen, County Roscommon, is a staff journalist with *The Irish Times*, specialising in financial and economic affairs. She is a graduate of University College Galway and University College Dublin. Before joining *The Irish Times*, she was Assistant Editor of *Finance Magazine* and has previously worked at Bank of Ireland Corporate Finance.

Lorna Siggins has been a staff journalist with *The Irish Times* since 1988, specialising in marine, environmental and development issues. Her reporting for that newspaper has ranged from North Sea oil rig accidents to the outbreak of civil war in Yugoslavia, famine in Somalia, an Everest expedition in Tibet and the United Nations Fourth Women's World Conference in Beijing.

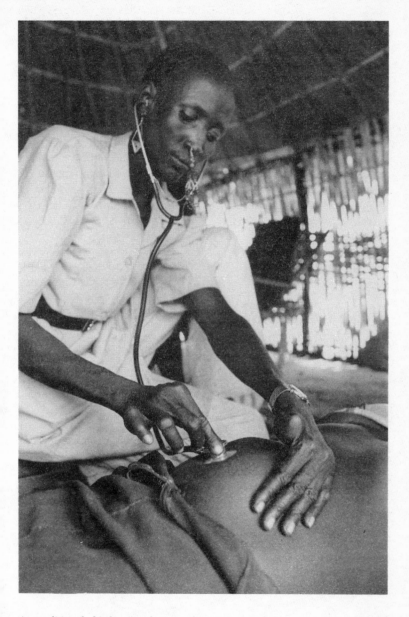

A traditional birth attendant working at an Oxfam-sponsored clinic in Agangrial, South Sudan. (Development Work in South Sudan: Obstacles and Opportunities by Deirdre Considine)

Photograph by Crispin Hughes.

Light After Darkness
An Experience of Nicaragua
Betty Purcell

Light After Darkness is an inspiring story of survival, optimism and courage. Betty Purcell writes personally and sensitively of her experiences in Nicaragua, of her work as a foreign reporter and on an international coffee brigade, of her travels through the countryside and her many fascinating encounters and conversations.

£4.95
ISBN: 1 946211 76 0

For a complete list of Attic Press Women's Studies titles, please contact us at

Attic Press
29, Upper Mount Street
Dublin 2
Ireland

Tel: (1 353) 661 6128   Fax: (1 353) 661 6176
E-mail: Atticirl@iol.ie   http://www.iol.ie/~atticirl/